OAE

English Language Arts Practice Questions

Mometrix

TEST PREPARATION

DEAR FUTURE EXAM SUCCESS STORY

First of all, **THANK YOU** for purchasing Mometrix study materials!

Second, congratulations! You are one of the few determined test-takers who are committed to doing whatever it takes to excel on your exam. **You have come to the right place.** We developed these practice tests with one goal in mind: to deliver you the best possible approximation of the questions you will see on test day.

Standardized testing is one of the biggest obstacles on your road to success, which only increases the importance of doing well in the high-pressure, high-stakes environment of test day. Your results on this test could have a significant impact on your future, and these practice tests will give you the repetitions you need to build your familiarity and confidence with the test content and format to help you achieve your full potential on test day.

Your success is our success

We would love to hear from you! If you would like to share the story of your exam success or if you have any questions or comments in regard to our products, please contact us at **800-673-8175** or **support@mometrix.com**.

Thanks again for your business and we wish you continued success!

Sincerely,
The Mometrix Test Preparation Team

Printed in the United States of America

Table of Contents

Practice Test #1

1. Regarding organization, what statement is most accurate about outlines relative to writing?

a. Outlining is only for student writers.
b. Outlines are for professional writers.
c. Outlines are for planning, not analyzing.
d. Outlines aid in planning and analysis.

2. Which of the following sentences has a complex structure?

a. Will finished the paper Friday, so he enjoyed the weekend.
b. As Will finished the paper on Friday, he enjoyed the weekend.
c. On Friday Will finished the paper and ended up enjoying the weekend.
d. Will finished the paper that was due Monday, and he enjoyed the weekend.

3. Which author is associated with the Contemporary movement?

a. Homer
b. Henry David Thoreau
c. George Orwell
d. William Shakespeare

4. Among these advantages of using digital media in education, which is most closely connected to reflecting individual differences among students?

a. Rapid navigation among multiple media
b. More diverse formats and experiences
c. Constant or frequent real-time updates
d. Global access to information and people

5. Archie says, "Northerners eat bland food." Which of the following terms most precisely describes the thought Archie expresses?

a. Stereotype
b. Inference
c. Assumption
d. Generalization

6. Which word is a definite article?

a. A
b. An
c. The
d. None of the above

7. Among genres of literature, which is typically the most condensed or verbally economical?

a. A play
b. A novel
c. A poem
d. An essay

8. The active reading strategy of text coding or text monitoring involves which of these?

a. Students separate codes into two columns.
b. Students write main points on sticky notes.
c. Students summarize a text in notation form.
d. Students make notes in the margins of a text.

9. Which of the following statements is correct regarding Standard English?

a. Standard English does not allow for variations of dialect.
b. Rules from standard English apply to written language.
c. Standard English is universal in English-speaking nations.
d. No standard English exists that is actually used in practice.

10. Which of the following statements best explains how students should choose a particular form of writing to fit their purpose?

a. Students who want to get readers to agree with them should use argumentative writing.
b. Students who want to tell a story and the lesson it affords should use speculative writing.
c. Students who want to invite readers to explore ideas should use descriptive writing.
d. Students who want to share an experience with readers should use informative writing.

11. A number of verb forms are used in headlines. These include simple tenses, infinitive forms, and auxiliary verbs dropped in the passive voice. Which headline below uses a simple tense?

a. LOST DOG RETURNS
b. GOVERNOR TO VISIT CITY
c. GRADUATE NAMED VALEDICTORIAN
d. HERO GIVEN AWARD

Refer to the following for questions 12–14:

(73) I should have been a pair of ragged claws
(74) Scuttling across the floors of silent seas.

(122) Shall I part my hair behind? Do I dare to eat a peach?
(123) I shall wear white flannel trousers, and walk upon the beach.
(124) I have heard the mermaids singing, each to each.
(125) I do not think that they will sing to me.

(129) We have lingered in the chambers of the sea
(130) By sea-girls wreathed with seaweed red and brown
(131) Till human voices wake us, and we drown.

12. Which of the following interpretations is most strongly supported by the excerpted lines?

a. The speaker loves the sea and wishes he or she could live in it.
b. The speaker's existence is as significant as the life of a crab.
c. The speaker had a near-death experience involving drowning.
d. The speaker was an accomplished diver but is now too old to dive.

13. Why does the speaker most likely say, "I do not think that they will sing to me"?

a. He does not feel at harmony with the ocean life around him.
b. He is in despair over his inadequacy next to the mermaids.
c. He feels that the mermaids would likely see him as an intruder.
d. He imagines that mermaids have no interest in singing to humans.

14. Which of the following interpretations of the final line is best supported by the excerpt?

a. Dreaming of mermaids is part of death by drowning.
b. Escapes to fantasy are ruined by the intrusion of reality.
c. Walking on the beach is peaceful until someone disturbs you.
d. Mermaids bewitch us from knowing that we drown.

15. Which of these accurately reflects a research-based strategy for writing instruction?

a. Brainstorming is a technique too open-ended for students planning writing.
b. Giving students steps to follow for argumentative writing is too structured.
c. Explicit instruction in planning, revision, and editing improves performance.
d. Collaborative writing deprives students of independently practicing writing.

16. Which of the following sentences is most likely to be a topic sentence of a paragraph?

a. Clearly, the time is ripe for a cultural shift where screens are seen as a necessary evil.
b. Already, increasing screen time has had disastrous effects on public health.
c. Finally, the most disturbing effects of screen time are seen in the realm of neuroscience.
d. Studies also note an unsettling correlation between developmental delay and screen time.

17. Which of the following literary elements are most likely to be found in both fictional narratives and nonfictional informational text?

a. The writing style of the author
b. Labeled diagrams and photos
c. Excitement and drama
d. Themes and plots

18. Which of the following is most accurate regarding the sequence of steps a reader should take to evaluate arguments in an informational text?

a. Readers should find supporting premises and only look for the conclusion once these are understood.
b. Readers should first identify an argument's conclusion and then identify the premises supporting it.
c. Readers should note an argument's conclusion and supporting premises in the order they are presented.
d. Readers should try to paraphrase premises to clarify them, not to make them fit with the conclusion.

19. If a student has a writing assignment, which of the following is true regarding his or her audience?

a. The student need not identify the audience because it is the teacher.
b. The student should consider the readers' purpose for reading and response to the writing.
c. The student should know his or her writing purpose and not be concerned with a reader's purposes.
d. The student can develop an audience profile but assume the main audience is the teacher.

20. "A tall man in a black raincoat and a yellow hat entered the restaurant, walked to the back, and sat down alone at the table farthest away from the staff and other patrons." This sentence has which of the following structures?

a. Simple
b. Complex
c. Compound
d. Compound-complex

21. What does a writer do in the organization stage?

a. Determines the purpose, thesis, and supporting details of the written work
b. Brainstorms ideas for items to include in the written work
c. Submits the writing to a classmate for editing
d. Writes the introduction and conclusion

22. Which of these is an example of poor focus that makes a paragraph ineffective?

a. Unclear transitions
b. Too few main ideas
c. Irrelevant sentences
d. A lack of solid evidence

23. Which of the following sentences uses tone and technical language that is appropriate for a scientific document such as a research paper?

a. Based on our analysis, we conclude that everyone needs this supplement.
b. This study has placed the compound's importance beyond any doubt.
c. As there are few reproducible assays, our findings are hardly significant.
d. We identified this compound as a central component of protein metabolism.

24. Which of the following techniques that writers can use to promote coherence in paragraphs best reinforces the importance of certain ideas?

a. Transition
b. Repetition
c. Parallelism
d. Consistency

25. Which of these is most accurate about the function of dialogue in fictional literature?

a. Dialogue can serve to advance the plot but not develop characters.
b. Dialogue can serve to illuminate themes and meanings and redirect plots.
c. Dialogue can serve to break up exposition and slow the pace of the story.
d. Dialogue can serve to reproduce real speech instead of adding drama.

26. In the sentence below, the expressions "to reflect" and "to enlighten" are examples of which of the following types of verbals?

> While set in the ancient and mythical world of Camelot, Tennyson's *Idylls of the King* often do more to reflect the Victorian issues of his day than to enlighten the reader about the world of King Arthur.

a. adverb
b. gerund
c. participle
d. infinitive

27. In the steps that a reader can follow to evaluate an informational text writer's arguments, which should come first?

a. Identifying the conclusion the argument makes
b. Judging the validity or supportiveness of premises
c. Clarifying premises or reasons with paraphrases
d. Identifying the supporting premises or reasons

28. Which of the following is true about the author's point of view in an informational text?

a. Readers can easily identify the author's point of view because informational texts include it as a main idea.
b. Readers often must infer the author's point of view because informational authors tend not to explicitly state it.
c. Readers may see the author's point of view equally well for neutral, balanced, and opinionated positions.
d. Readers who must analyze a text to identify the author's point of view can assume the text is poorly written.

Refer to the following for question 29:

> A class considers the paragraph below:
>
> Sarah and Kelly grinned at one another conspiratorially as they approached Dad, who was quietly reading his paper in the living room. "Dad, we'd like to ride our bikes down to Emil's house today," giggled Kelly. She glanced at her sister and shifted her weight from foot to foot. Dad appeared to think this over for a moment and replied, "Sure, that's fine with me!" The girls scampered to get their bikes and were soon on their way. With the children gone, Dad noticed how peaceful and quiet the house sounded. His reverie was quickly interrupted as he heard Mom calling from upstairs, "okay, everybody, I told you at breakfast that I need as much help as I can get to help me give the dog a bath, clean the house and finish the laundry today!" Dad groaned, knowing that he had been conned!

29. Which method would be best for helping students determine the meaning of the word "reverie" in the next to last sentence?

a. Using context clues
b. Making an educated guess
c. Decoding the prefix, root, and suffix of the word
d. Previewing and reviewing

30. "To better serve you, we ask that you answer this short survey, it will take less than five minutes." Which common grammatical/mechanical error(s) does this sentence include? Select ALL correct answers.

a. The sentence employs inconsistent verb tense.
b. The sentence has a split infinitive.
c. The sentence contains a comma splice.
d. There is a misplaced modifier.
e. There are no errors.

Refer to the following for questions 31–34:

> It was the best of times, it was the worst of times, it was the age of wisdom, it was the age of foolishness, it was the epoch of belief, it was the epoch of incredulity, it was the season of Light, it was the season of Darkness, it was the spring of hope, it was the winter of despair, we had everything before us, we had nothing before us, we were all going direct to heaven, we were all going direct the other way – in short, the period was so far like the present period, that some of its noisiest authorities insisted on its being received, for good or for evil, in the superlative degree of comparison only.
>
> Excerpted from *A Tale of Two Cities* by Charles Dickens (1859)

31. Which of the following ideas did Dickens want to convey in this introduction?

a. The extreme good and bad described were only imagined by "authorities."
b. Everything could seem to be best or worst depending on the individual.
c. The past era described was indistinguishable from the present one.
d. The readers' present era and this past era both had good and bad.

32. Of the following statements, which accurately describes textual evidence of Dickens's techniques and their effects?

a. The rhythm and anaphora reinforce the idea of equal and opposing forces.
b. The presentation of multiple pairs of opposites introduces a paradox motif.
c. The author's use of anastrophe and rhythm emphasizes contrasting opposites.
d. The author uses repetition to slow the pacing of the story.

33. Among the following, which pair is most figurative in meaning?

a. Wisdom and foolishness
b. Belief and incredulity
c. Light and darkness
d. Hope and despair

34. From reading only this introductory paragraph, what can readers infer about the rest of this novel?

a. The story will likely include equal amounts of good and bad.
b. The story will likely focus more on bad than good.
c. The story will likely explain how good and bad are really the same.
d. The story will likely show how good can come from bad.

35. Which of the following is true regarding critical evaluation of books and articles?

a. Historical perspectives are not applicable to judging books.
b. Consider if journals contain advertising and, if so, for what.
c. Information in books is generally assumed to be out of date.
d. Book reviews should be avoided as they may introduce bias.

36. Which of the following instructional strategies would likely help students the most in understanding the difference between denotation and connotation and help them learn to identify the connotation of a word in context?

a. Providing example sentences in multiple choice questions asking for a word's connotation
b. Filling out a Venn diagram with sets of words that have connotations, denotations, or both
c. Assigning a reading where students identify and highlight words that have connotations
d. Giving word definitions and asking students to describe the feelings elicited by each definition

37. In "The Story of an Hour" by Kate Chopin (1894), in which of these does the author use the plot structure element of discourse, including sequence and selection, to augment reader surprise at the story's outcome?

a. Narrating some events out of their chronological order
b. Omitting some details, like Brently Mallard's trip home
c. Omitting all description of Louise, letting actions speak
d. Options (A) and (B), but not (C)

38. Authors of technical informational text may need to write in nontechnical language for which of the following reasons?

a. To communicate denser content rather than clear messages
b. To inform other professionals working in relevant fields
c. To present effective proposals that secure funding for projects to people or organizations who may or may not be familiar with the subject matter
d. To explain concepts to a select few experts

39. Another name for a persuasive essay is:

a. Dynamic essay
b. Convincing essay
c. Argumentative essay
d. Position paper

40. Of the following variations, which one is a simple sentence?

a. "You could run but could not hide."
b. "Although you can run, you can't hide."
c. "You can run, but you cannot hide."
d. "Run; run fast, because you can't hide."

41. According to MLA citation guidelines, which source-specific details should be included for both print and electronic sources: the publisher for books and the periodical title, volume, issue, and page numbers when available for periodical articles?

a. Publisher name
b. Periodical name, volume, issue, page numbers
c. Publisher name for books and periodical title, volume, issue, and page numbers when available for periodical articles, whether the sources are print or electronic
d. Database name, database publisher name, URL

42. Which of the following criteria is used to evaluate the credibility of a text as a research source?

a. The text contains no outdated information.
b. The text underwent the process of peer review.
c. The text speaks for itself in terms of its value and relevance.
d. The text was published by an organization that most people know.

43. The following is an excerpt from William Blake's 1794 poem "The Tyger":

Tyger Tyger, burning bright,
In the forests of the night;
What immortal hand or eye,
Could frame thy fearful symmetry?

In what distant deeps or skies.
Burnt the fire of thine eyes?
On what wings dare he aspire?
What the hand, dare seize the fire?

Which of the following questions does the poet seem to be asking in this poem?

a. Can anyone grasp a tiger's power?
b. What makes the tiger seem so fearsome?
c. What power could have created the tiger?
d. How did the tiger come to be a feared animal?

44. In an essay, which part of the introduction should come first?

a. The thesis statement
b. A hook
c. Background on the essay's purpose
d. A preview of the essay's structure

45. Of the following, which is NOT common in both satire and realism?

a. Irony
b. Serious tone
c. Exaggeration
d. Vernacular dialogue

46. In a paired reading activity to practice identifying main ideas and details in an informational text, what are the paired students normally asked to do?

a. Take turns reading aloud
b. Read aloud at the same time
c. Read the same part of the text silently
d. Read different parts of the text silently

47. Which of the following is critically effective for the purposes and audiences of blog writing?

a. Writing with correct punctuation
b. Writing with longer paragraphs
c. Writing with longer sentences
d. Writing with smaller font size

48. Of the following, which statement is true about instruction in the alphabetic principle?

a. Letter-sound relationships with the highest utility should be the earliest ones introduced.
b. The instruction of letter-sound correspondences should always be done in word context.
c. Letter-sound relationship practice times should only be assigned apart from other lessons.
d. Letter-sound relationship practice should focus on new relationships, not go over old ones.

49. When writing an essay, which of the following tasks is best to complete first?

a. List all details supporting each main point
b. Decide how to sequence main points
c. Organize details in a logical order
d. Narrow possible topics down to one main idea

Refer to the following for question 50:

> I bequeath myself to the dirt to grow from the grass I love,
> If you want me again look for me under your boot-soles.

50. Which of the following interpretations is most strongly supported by the excerpted lines?

a. The persona feels at one with nature even in dying.
b. The persona sees themselves at a low station in life.
c. The persona is facing the grim reality of being buried.
d. The persona wants to show how that he or she feels "stepped on."

51. "This treatise developed from an initial idea like a plant develops from a seed." The preceding sentence is an example of which literary device and argument method?

a. Analogy
b. Allegory
c. Allusion
d. Antithesis

52. What is correct about how teachers can use rubrics as a research-based assessment method?

a. Teachers should use rubrics to conduct formative (not summative) student work assessments.
b. Teachers should use rubrics for lesson objectives, both to guide and to assess students' work.
c. Teachers should use rubrics to conduct summative (not formative) student work assessments.
d. Teachers should use rubrics in place of stating learning objectives and modeling performance.

53. Among these literary genres, in which pair has one *most* been used within the other?

a. Nonfiction prose within poetry
b. Fictional prose within drama
c. Poetry within fictional drama
d. Poetry within nonfiction prose

54. The sentence, "After completing the assignment correctly, the teacher gave Peter a high grade" is an example of which kind of error?

a. A lack of parallelism
b. A sentence fragment
c. A dangling participle
d. A run-on sentence

55. When incorporating outside sources into a research paper, which of these should students do?

a. End papers with quotations
b. Include more brief quotations
c. Include many longer quotations
d. Quote only supporting information

56. What is the purpose of an adverb in a sentence?

a. It identifies a person, place, or thing
b. It describes an action or state of being
c. It modifies a verb, adjective, or adverb
d. It describes or otherwise modifies a noun

57. Collaborative Strategic Reading (CSR) is a teaching technique that depends on two teaching practices. These practices are:

a. Cooperative learning and reading comprehension
b. Cooperative reading and metacognition
c. Reading comprehension and metacognition
d. Cooperative learning and metacognition

58. Which of the following parts of speech forms or starts the predicate of a sentence?

a. Verb
b. Noun
c. Adjective
d. Adverb

59. Which type of poetic form is characterized by three lines in free verse that contain a total of 17 syllables, with each line frequently having five, seven, and five syllables, respectively?

a. Haiku
b. Sonnet
c. Limerick
d. Cinquain

60. In Edgar Allan Poe's story *The Tell-Tale Heart,* which of the following is NOT a way in which Poe develops the theme of madness and paranoia?

a. The narrator's admission of insanity
b. The narrator's casual lack of remorse
c. The narrator's fixation on the "eye"
d. The narrator's perception of sound

61. Which of the following is a key difference between writing a journalistic article and writing an academic essay?

a. An essay should attempt to persuade the reader, but a news article should seek to entertain.
b. An essay should use formal and objective wording, but a news article should have a friendly, casual tone.
c. An essay may begin with a hook, but a news article should give important information first.
d. An essay should present information about a particular topic, but a news article should relate to current events.

62. A class reads an essay about the benefits to youth of pet ownership. The author's position is very clear: she believes young people should be given the responsibility of taking care of pets. The author cites facts, research studies, and statistics to strengthen her position. This type of writing is called:

a. Expository
b. Narrative
c. Persuasive
d. Didactic

Refer to the following for questions 63–64:

> Call the roller of big cigars,
> The muscular one, and bid him whip
> In kitchen cups concupiscent curds.
> Let the wenches dawdle in such dress
> As they are used to wear, and let the boys
> Bring flowers in last month's newspapers.
> Let be be finale of seem.
> The only emperor is the emperor of ice-cream.

63. Which literary device is shown in the third line of the excerpted stanza?

a. Alliteration
b. Hyperbole
c. Onomatopoeia
d. Metonymy

64. Which of the following most closely restates the meaning of line 7, "Let be be finale of seem"?

a. Let harsh realities turn into peaceful acceptance.
b. Let life for the moment seem better than it really is.
c. Let yourself appreciate the good before facing the bad.
d. Let the way things seem become the way things really are.

65. Which of the following statements accurately describes the two sentences below?

(1) "The man with a broken arm sat in a chair." (2) "The man sat in a chair with a broken arm."

a. Each sentence has a different meaning, as shown by its syntax.
b. One of the sentences has an unclear meaning due to its syntax.
c. Both sentences have unclear meanings because of their syntax.
d. The sentences have the same meaning but use different syntax.

66. A four-year-old child who does not correctly or clearly produce the speech sounds /r/ and /s/:

a. Likely has delayed language development
b. Likely has normal articulatory development
c. Likely has some degree of hearing impairment
d. Likely needs early intervention for stuttering

67. Which of the following statements is true regarding screening and diagnostic assessments?

a. Screening assessments provide more thorough information than diagnostic assessments about students' specific strengths and needs.
b. Screening assessments are typically used to confirm diagnostic assessment results.
c. Screening assessments are used to identify students who may be at future risk of academic difficulties and may benefit from interventions.
d. Diagnostic assessments are used to identify students who may be at future risk of academic difficulties and may benefit from interventions.

68. Research studies reveal that teaching self-regulation skills to students improves their writing skills. Which of the following statements is true about this relationship?

a. Teaching self-regulation makes students' writing efforts less strategic and more natural.
b. Teaching self-regulation improves students' awareness of their own strengths and weaknesses.
c. Teaching self-regulation reduces students' emotional, cognitive, and behavioral inhibitions.
d. Teaching self-regulation enables students to work within the confines of writing strategies.

69. When writing an essay, which of the following attributes belongs in the introduction?

a. Getting the reader's attention
b. Developing the thesis statement
c. Giving examples of the thesis idea
d. Giving the reader a sense of closure

70. Which of the following statements about inferences is accurate regarding any given informational text?

a. They enable readers to recall specific details from the text.
b. They help readers to fill in information not stated in the text.
c. They require readers to first understand the entirety of the text.
d. They force readers to articulate questions they have about the text.

71. Which of these statements is true of informational text comprehension?

a. It relies entirely on retrieving important information.
b. It depends on the reader's indirect reasoning ability alone.
c. It requires the reader to recall information and make inferences.
d. It includes inferences made by the reader but not their prior knowledge.

Refer to the following for question 72:

Poem by Emily Dickinson:

"There's a Certain Slant of Light"

There's a certain slant of light,
On winter afternoons,
That oppresses, like the weight
Of cathedral tunes.
Heavenly hurt it gives us;
We can find no scar,
But internal difference
Where the meanings are.
None may teach it anything,
'Tis the seal, despair,—
An imperial affliction
Sent us of the air.
When it comes, the landscape listens,
Shadows hold their breath;
When it goes, 'tis like the distance
On the look of death.

72. Which poetic device is used in the following lines?

"When it comes, the landscape listens, / Shadows hold their breath;"

a. Assonance
b. Personification
c. Simile
d. Metaphor

73. Identify the stylistic error in the following sentence:

There is no reason to loudly shout your answers.

a. Lack of parallelism
b. Split infinitive
c. Squinting modifier
d. Subject-verb disagreement

74. Which of the following sentences uses metaphor to create figurative meanings?

a. He became a tiger in the boxing ring, but he turned into a pussycat at dinner afterward.
b. He was like a tiger in the boxing ring, but later during dinner, he was just like a pussycat.
c. He fought so fiercely in the boxing ring, but afterward at dinner he was gentle and kind.
d. He was ferocious when he was boxing, but he was sweet and gentle in social situations.

75. Which strategy can be used to build readers' confidence and increase both comprehension and fluency when introducing an unknown text?

a. Introducing new vocabulary before reading
b. Reading the first few pages aloud before asking students to finish it independently
c. Listing what students want to learn about the topic
d. Asking students to predict what the text will be about based on the title and cover

76. Which of the following best demonstrates writing appropriately for a specific task, purpose, and audience?

a. Using jargon in a book report that will be read aloud to classmates
b. Using simple language when describing a new procedure to expert colleagues
c. Using vivid, entertaining language when writing a story for young students
d. Using humor to request new privileges from one's parents

77. Which of the following is the cognitive or learning objective of an assignment that asks students to "describe," "explain," "summarize," "restate," "classify," or "review" material they have read?

a. Knowledge recall
b. Application
c. Comprehension
d. Evaluation

78. Which of the following would NOT be important to consider when evaluating the conciseness of a speech?

a. The amount of time the speaker takes to pause before answering questions
b. Whether or not interesting information is prioritized over necessary information
c. The number of details and anecdotes that are given to keep the audience engaged
d. How long the speaker takes to make a point or answer a question

79. What can syntax almost always help a reader deduce about an unfamiliar word in a sentence?

a. The word's meaning
b. The word's part of speech
c. Both the word's meaning and its part of speech
d. Neither the word's meaning nor its part of speech

80. Which of the following common modes of writing is most characterized by the author's assumption of certain facts or truths?

a. Informative
b. Descriptive
c. Persuasive
d. Narrative

81. Among instructional strategies that aid in student comprehension of nonfictional text, which of these is most useful for promoting critical thinking?

a. Answering open-ended questions about texts
b. Skimming the text for features that give signs
c. Establishing connections between text and life
d. Establishing connections between text and self

82. Public speakers want to give speeches that make their audience pay attention, but they also want to give speeches whose messages are meaningful enough to remain in audience member's minds. This can best be accomplished with:

a. Simple language and stories
b. Strict logical progression
c. Sophisticated language and ideas
d. Eye contact

83. Identify the grammatical error in the following sentence:

She said, "Give it to me quick!"

a. Dangling participle
b. Split infinitive
c. Adjective/adverb confusion
d. Misplaced modifier

84. What structural pattern in a paragraph serves to show readers instead of telling them?

a. Narration
b. Description
c. Classification
d. Giving examples

85. William Shakespeare wrote during which historical and literary period?

a. Medieval
b. Renaissance
c. Restoration
d. Enlightenment

86. Which of the following considerations does NOT help readers infer the author's point of view or purpose in informational text where it is not explicitly stated?

a. What the author wants to accomplish by writing the text
b. How effective the author's selection and use of supporting evidence is
c. What the author wants to persuade readers to accept, agree with, or believe
d. How the author's word choice affects the reader's perceptions of the subject matter

87. "He woke up, looked at the clock, got dressed, ate a hurried breakfast, got into his car, drove downtown, parked the car, walked across the street and up the block to the corner building next to the grocery store, opened the front door, and went inside." What type of sentence is this?

a. Compound–complex
b. Compound sentence
c. A complex sentence
d. A simple sentence

88. A word's part of speech can be recognizable, even if it's meaning is unknown. In the sentence below, what is the part of speech of the word *trouvère,* based on its context in the following sentence?

Many of the Arthurian legends are believed to have come from the writings of twelfth-century *trouvère* Chretien de Troyes.

a. noun
b. verb
c. adjective
d. adverb

89. Which statement is most accurate regarding journals as a form of writing?

a. Journals are only for confiding and processing personal experiences in private.
b. Journals entries should all open with a greeting.
c. Journals can serve as free practice for writers to develop their skills.
d. Journals may best serve as a therapy for the reader but not for the author.

90. Authors Annie Sebold in *The Lovely Bones* and Markus Zusak in *The Book Thief* both use which of these viewpoints or voices to narrate their novels?

a. The third-person omniscient narrator
b. The first-person omniscient narrator
c. The first-person limited narrator
d. The third-person limited narrator

91. Identify the grammatical error in the following sentence:

He found it easier to more efficiently complete the form online.

a. Dangling participle
b. Split infinitive
c. Adjective/adverb confusion
d. Misplaced modifier

92. Which of the following terms refers to description that activates the reader's senses?

a. Simile
b. Imagery
c. Metaphor
d. Hyperbole

93. Young children tend to learn vocabulary more effectively when under certain levels of demand. Which of the following best represents an appropriate use of demand for activities made to support acquisition of new vocabulary words?

a. Teachers alternate between low-demand and high-demand questions.
b. Teachers employ new vocabulary in clear contexts, but do not provide direct support.
c. Teachers restrict their questions to those with low complexity until students demonstrate mastery.
d. Teachers move from low-demand question to high-demand ones.

94. Which of the following does NOT involve a reader evaluating the methods of appeal used by the author of a text?

a. Paraphrasing, summarizing, or outlining the text
b. Determining a method of appeal that would be better
c. Researching the topic along with unfamiliar vocabulary
d. Considering the types of appeals the author uses and why

95. Which of these is NOT a benefit of a well-organized essay?

a. A well-organized essay is more likely to gain readers' acceptance of its thesis as valid.
b. A well-organized essay is more likely to hold readers' attention.
c. A well-organized essay requires less effort to write but more effort to read and understand.
d. A well-organized essay makes it easier for readers to identify the main ideas and the evidence that supports them.

96. Among the following sets of transition phrases, which is best for indicating the presence of another supporting detail when one supporting detail has already been provided?

a. *However, although, whereas, but*
b. *In fact, indeed, surprisingly, interestingly*
c. *For example, such as, to demonstrate, for instance*
d. *Moreover, furthermore, additionally, not only ... but also*

97. A sentence with two independent and two dependent clauses would be most accurately classified as which of the following?

a. Simple
b. Complex
c. Compound
d. Compound–complex

98. In his epic poem *The Song of Hiawatha* (1855), how does Henry Wadsworth Longfellow most use poetic devices?

a. He uses couplets to answer questions asked before.
b. He uses couplets to clarify development of a theme.
c. He uses meter that evokes the rhythms of chanting.
d. He uses irony to help in development of the theme.

99. Scholars have identified three major categories of connections that students make when reading: text-to-self connections, text-to-world connections, and text-to-text connections. Which of the following student statements is an example of a connection of text to the world?

a. These mythic gods have more power but feel and act like humans.
b. This novel is set during a period I learned about in my history textbook.
c. I can relate to how the main character felt about being controlled.
d. The protagonist reminds me of the main character in another story.

100. A telecommunications salesman is writing informational text to persuade customers to agree to buy the products and services he is selling. One tactic includes advising the customer, "You are hemorrhaging money!" This is an example of which method of persuasion?

a. A generalization
b. Using a metaphor
c. Rhetorical question
d. Negative connotation

101. When a middle school student needs to determine whether written sentences in a worksheet are complete and correct for an assignment, which paper or digital reference material should s/he consult?

a. A paper or a digital encyclopedia
b. A physical or an online dictionary
c. A paper or digital grammar guide
d. A word-processor grammar check

102. Which of the following statements is correct regarding effective speech delivery?

a. Speakers should avoid practicing speeches to appear spontaneous.
b. Verbal and nonverbal communication should seem equally natural.
c. Speakers should avoid using humor because it will distract the audience.
d. Random movements can help sustain the attention of the audience.

103. Maria's topic sentence is: "My family throws elaborate holiday celebrations." Which of the following would be the best supporting detail to follow that sentence?

a. Holidays are just a waste of everyone's time and money, in my opinion.
b. First, we decide who will host the holiday dinner and when the celebration will take place.
c. My household includes five people, but my extended family includes over thirty people.
d. Afterwards, we all help clean up and then relax by continuing to chat with each other.

104. Mr. Ank has a game he plans to play with his middle school English students today. He has recorded several commercials from television and will play them without sound for the students. After each silent commercial, the students will share their ideas about what product the commercial is advertising. Following this game, the class will participate in a follow-up discussion and exercise. What is the likely purpose of Mr. Ank's game?

a. To turn his students into savvy consumers.
b. To help students understand how visual images affect meaning and understanding.
c. To demonstrate how students can use visual images in their own schoolwork.
d. To introduce variation into his instruction and give the kids a fun activity.

105. Which statement is accurate regarding guidelines for searching when conducting a literature review for writing a research paper?

a. Too many references indicate the research question is not narrow enough.
b. Too few references indicate the area of investigation is not specific enough.
c. No references at all indicate the topic and research question must be invalid.
d. Writers should search for references before determining the topic of their research paper.

106. What is the general purpose of the *roman à clef* form in novels and other literature?

a. To give readers a greater challenge in understanding
b. To disguise truths too threatening to state explicitly
c. To confuse readers deliberately by hiding meanings
d. To distance readers from traumatic experiences

107. Which of the following statements most accurately compares the components of speeches and the components of essays?

a. Speeches and essays have similar introductions.
b. Speeches provide supporting evidence in greater detail than essays do.
c. The conclusion of a speech must be more forceful and engaging than the conclusion of an essay.
d. Speeches may include greetings, mentions of honored guests, and thanks, but essays should not include these elements.

108. Suppose someone writes an expository essay arguing against legalizing one specific drug, basing this argument on the premise that its legalization will lead to more and more drugs being legalized until no drugs are illegal anymore. Which of the following logical fallacies has this writer committed?

a. Slippery slope
b. Non sequitur
c. Red herring
d. Straw man

109. Which of the following statements is accurate regarding criteria for evaluating the credibility of websites as sources?

a. Who publishes or sponsors a web page is more important than its domain name.
b. Whether information can be verified supersedes the timeliness of page updates.
c. Users must be vigilant against writer and publisher bias.
d. Links to, citations of, and recommendations for other sources take away credibility.

110. An informational text states that a Yugoslavian nationalist assassinated Austria-Hungary's heir to the throne, Archduke Franz Ferdinand; this triggered a diplomatic crisis, wherein Austria-Hungary issued the Kingdom of Serbia an ultimatum; in reaction to this ultimatum, a number of previously formed international alliances were then reinforced; and therefore within several weeks, the major world powers had gone to war; consequently, the fighting soon spread worldwide. This is an example of which kind of structural or organizational pattern?

a. Descriptive
b. Cause and effect
c. Sequence and order
d. Comparison-contrast

111. "After David met Marcia, he knew she was the one, and he soon proposed marriage to her." This is what type of sentence?

a. It is a compound sentence.
b. It is a compound–complex sentence.
c. It is a complex sentence.
d. It is a simple sentence.

112. Use the following sentence to answer this question.

After we arrive, we will split up into small groups to tour the museum separately.

In this sentence, which part is a prepositional phrase?

a. after we arrive
b. split up
c. into small groups
d. to tour

113. According to MLA guidelines for writing research papers, which of the following is correct regarding citations of sources found on the internet if the author's name cannot be found quickly on the source page or site?

a. Assume the author is not named, as this is a common occurrence on the internet.
b. Name an agency or corporation as the author if it is the publisher of the source.
c. Author names are often on websites, but sometimes they are hard to find.
d. It is not permissible to cite the book or article title in lieu of an author's name.

114. Identify the grammatical error in the following sentence:

Children who hug seldom are shy.

a. Lack of parallelism
b. Split infinitive
c. Squinting modifier
d. Subject-verb disagreement

115. Author Frances O'Roark Dowell used a late 1920s Appalachian Mountain regional dialect in her award-winning novel *Dovey Coe* (2000) for the narration. Why might she have done this?

a. The author is most comfortable speaking in this dialect
b. This dialect was natural to the setting and the narrator
c. The unusual language would attract readers' attention
d. It contrasted with the characters, establishing tension

116. Which of the following most accurately defines information literacy?

a. The set of skills required for reading and comprehending information
b. The set of skills necessary to amass a comprehensive base of knowledge
c. The set of skills required for the finding, retrieval, analysis, and use of information
d. The set of skills necessary for effectively communicating information to others

117. The first paragraph of Abraham Lincoln's Gettysburg Address is a single sentence that reads: "Four score and seven years ago our fathers brought forth, on this continent, a new nation, conceived in Liberty, and dedicated to the proposition that all men are created equal." In the two-column notes active reading strategy, which of the following phrases from this introduction would go in the main idea column?

a. "Four score and seven years ago"
b. "...our fathers brought forth... a new nation"
c. "...conceived in Liberty"
d. "...dedicated to the proposition that all men are created equal."

118. The syllable *-tion* is a(n) _____ and turns a _____ into a _____.

a. suffix; verb; noun
b. affix; noun; pronoun
c. prefix; noun; verb
d. infix; noun; adjective

119. Which author's works have explored the experience and roles of black women in American society?

a. Toni Morrison
b. Washington Irving
c. Richard Wright
d. Flannery O'Conner

120. Which statement about the relationship between conflict and plot is most accurate?

a. Conflict is what drives the plot of a story forward.
b. Resolving the main conflict is often not the protagonist's primary endeavor.
c. Emotional, mental, and moral conflicts impact plot less than physical conflicts do.
d. The climax of a plot only occurs after the main conflict has been resolved.

121. In his *Poetics*, Aristotle defines epic, comic, and tragic poetry genres. Subsequent scholars have altered these somewhat. Which three main poetry genres have they defined?

a. Epic, lyric, and dramatic poetry
b. Epic, comic, and tragic poetry
c. Dramatic, comic, and tragic
d. Lyric, tragic, and comedic

122. Read the sentence below and use it to answer this question.

Because he was late, he missed the field trip, and this caused him to fail the class.

How many dependent and independent clauses does this sentence contain?

a. One dependent clause and one independent clause
b. Two dependent clauses and one independent clause
c. One dependent clause and two independent clauses
d. Two dependent clauses and two independent clauses

123. In *Romeo and Juliet,* Shakespeare writes Romeo's line, "What light from yonder window breaks?" What is the syntax of this sentence?

a. Subject-object-verb
b. Subject-verb-object
c. Object-subject-verb
d. Verb-object-subject

124. Which of the following is an appropriate criterion to consider when evaluating a student's summary of a passage from literature?

a. The summary should be concise, even at the expense of completeness.
b. The summary should include the reactions and opinions the reader had.
c. The summary should cover points in proportion to the reader's interest.
d. The summary should tag attributions, cite sources, and limit quotations.

125. For evaluating the credibility of a source when doing research, which of these is true?

a. The author's reputation is more important than whether s/he cites sources.
b. The source should always be as recent as possible, regardless of the subject.
c. The author's point of view and/or purpose is not relevant to the credibility.
d. The kinds of sources various audiences value influences credibility for them.

126. Which of these is a correct statement about how to use a rubric in teaching writing?

a. Teachers should encourage students to use the rubric as a guide in what and how to write.
b. The teacher should not explain the rubric to students in advance.
c. Rubrics are solely for teachers to use in assessing student writing.
d. Teachers should only use rubrics for organizing their lesson plans.

127. Which of the following is a primary source?

a. A report of an original research experiment
b. An academic textbook's citation of research
c. A quotation of a researcher in a news article
d. A website description of another's research

128. Which of the following is true about how teachers should use formal and informal instruments for formative assessment in the classroom?

a. Teachers should use multiple formal and informal assessments as bases for student grouping.
b. Teachers should use only formal test instruments for conducting their formative assessments.
c. Teachers should select one specific formal or informal assessment instrument to use exclusively.
d. Teachers should use formative assessments only for evaluating students, not for teaching them.

129. If students in middle school grades are assigned to write text for students in early elementary grades to read, which of the following should they do?

a. Use script handwriting rather than printing to set examples for the readers.
b. Use vocabulary, sentence structure, and handwriting on the readers' levels.
c. Use longer, more complex sentences to provide a challenge for the readers.
d. Use their usual vocabulary, sentence structure, and handwriting as is natural.

130. Writers of informational texts use various structures to organize and present their ideas. Which pattern of organization is suggested by the appearance of such words and phrases as *because, therefore, as a result, for this reason,* and *consequently*?

a. Comparison and contrast
b. Problem and solution
c. Cause and effect
d. Temporal sequence

Answer Key and Explanations for Test #1

1. D: Outlines benefit students (A) and professional writers (B), not only one or the other. The main point(s) of a paragraph or an entire piece, and the details that support the main point(s), can be more quickly identified in outlines that summarize them in single sentences than they can by reading through all the additional language of a fully developed piece. Outlines can be used not only to plan writing (C), but also to analyze existing writing (D). Readers (or writers reviewing their own work) can make outlines to summarize the main point/idea in one sentence, and then list and number the supporting details, also each in a single sentence.

2. B: The sentence in choice B contains one dependent clause (*As Will finished the paper on Friday*) and one independent clause (*he enjoyed the weekend*). This exemplifies complex structure, so choice B is correct. Choice A is incorrect because it contains a sentence with compound structure—two independent clauses joined by a comma followed by a coordinating conjunction. Choice C is incorrect because this sentence has a simple structure. Though it has two main verbs in parallel (and therefore a compound predicate), it has only one independent clause and no dependent clauses because it only has one subject. Choice D is incorrect because this sentence has a compound-complex structure, with two independent clauses and one dependent clause (the relative clause *that was due Monday*).

3. C: Authors of the Contemporary movement wrote from 1945 to the present. George Orwell wrote *Animal Farm* in 1945 and *1984* in 1949.

4. B: Choice B is correct because differences among individual students are addressed very effectively by the diversity of formats and experiences available in digital media. Choice A is incorrect because the ability to navigate rapidly among various media is an advantage to all students and does not support individual differences. Choice C is similarly incorrect because the timeliness of updates in digital media are advantageous for all students. Choice D is incorrect because global access to information and people (such as experts, mentors, and peers) is, again, an advantage for every student and teacher.

5. A: The thought behind this statement is most precisely described as a stereotype, so choice A is correct. A stereotype is an assumption or generalization made about everybody in an identified group. The other answer choices are accurate descriptions of the thought that the statement expresses; however, they are less precise. An inference (B) is a conclusion based on available evidence rather than a conclusion arrived at through logical deduction. The statement in question is not necessarily an inference, so choice B is incorrect. The statement does reflect an assumption (C), but there are many kinds of assumptions aside from stereotypes. Likewise, the statement is certainly a generalization (D), but generalizations can be made about anything, while this one pertains to a specific group of people, so it is more precisely described as a stereotype.

6. C: *The* is a definite article because it refers to a specific noun. *A* (A) and *an* (B) are indefinite articles, which refer to nonspecific nouns. For example, "Let's read *a* book" means let's read any book; "Let's read *the* book" means let's read a certain, specified book. Therefore, answer choice D is incorrect.

7. C: Poems are typically the most condensed or economical in their use of words. Plays (A), typically more condensed in language than novels because more of the story is told directly through actions which novels must verbally describe, are still not as condensed as poems because they contain more dialogue. Novels (B) are full-length books, by definition longer than short stories, novelettes, or novellas; they often elaborate more about plot and character development than many poems, thus using more words. They also more often use complete sentences throughout, whereas poems may use phrases in addition to/instead of sentences. Essays (D) tend to expound on nonfictional topics in prose; hence, although they are far shorter than novels, they use many more words to express ideas than plays or most poems.

8. D: In the active reading strategy of text coding or text monitoring, students write preset codes to note their comprehension status in the margins of the text or on sticky notes, so choice D is correct. Choice A is incorrect as text coding does not involve students separating codes into columns—a technique used in the two-column notes reading strategy. Choice B is incorrect because text coding may involve writing codes, instead of main points, on sticky notes. Choice C is incorrect as text coding does not involve summarizing a text.

9. B: The term standard English refers to a form of English used in an English-speaking country that is reflected in dictionaries and grammar books, taught to English language learners, used in published writing, and so on. Because the rules of standard English are adhered to mainly in edited writing, choice B is correct. Standard English actually includes and allows for a range of dialects, which is exemplified by the fact that what is considered a standard English varies between English-speaking countries, so choice A is incorrect. Standard English is not universal; different English-speaking countries have different standard Englishes, so choice C is incorrect. Choice D is incorrect because edited and published writing generally adheres to some form of standard English.

10. A: Choice A is correct because students who want to get readers to agree with them should use argumentation or persuasion. Students who want to relate a story and the lesson to learn from it should use narrative writing, not speculative writing, so choice B is incorrect. Students who want to invite readers to explore ideas should use speculative writing, not descriptive writing, so choice C is incorrect. Students wanting to share an experience with readers should use descriptive or narrative writing depending on the experience, not informative writing, so choice D is incorrect.

11. A: This headline uses the simple tense. In this case, it's the simple present tense. B uses the infinitive form, while C and D both drop the auxiliary verb in the passive voice.

12. B: Throughout this excerpt, there is evidence that the speaker feels a sense of paralysis over seemingly inconsequential decisions (as in "Do I dare to eat a peach") and that they feel they would have been better off born as something else, even something as insignificant as "a pair of ragged claws." On the whole, the excerpt suggests that the persona speaking views their own existence as on the same level of value as that of a crab, so choice B is correct. Though there is evidence that the persona likes the sea, and they speak as if they are fascinated by the life in it, this does not seem to be the source of their discontentment, so choice A is incorrect. The persona mentions drowning in the final line of the excerpt (which is also the final line of the poem), but there is no evidence that they are looking back on a trauma of the past, so choice C is incorrect. Similarly, there is no evidence that they are a diver, though they claim to have "lingered" in the depths of the ocean (perhaps figuratively or in fantasy), so choice D is incorrect.

13. B: The persona's feeling of inadequacy is evident in the first three lines of the excerpt, particularly in "I should have been a pair of ragged claws." The line "I do not think that they will sing to me" seems to match the feeling of inadequacy expressed in these lines, and it further frames the feeling by suggesting that the speaker is not worthy to hear the beautiful singing. Choice B is, therefore, the best answer. While choice A could be true, the speaker's apparent admiration for the sea and the life in it does not suggest that the speaker is trying to express any lack of harmony with the sea. Choices C and D might both be plausible, but there is no evidence in the excerpt to support these interpretations.

14. B: Though the last line is open to interpretation, choice B is the best supported among the choices available. Hearing the mermaids singing to each other seems to be a fantasy of the persona, given that the persona themselves and the audience know that mermaids are not real. Furthermore, the awakening from this fantasy into a world where the persona feels quite insignificant would be a harsh awakening indeed. There is no evidence to support the interpretation in choice A, and it seems unlikely that a refined, modern speaker would be trying to tell the audience this. Choice C is plausible, but the walk on the beach does not seem pleasant for the persona; instead it seems to further confront them with their own inadequacies. There is no evidence in this excerpt to support the interpretation in choice D.

15. C: Research finds brainstorming effective to help students plan writing (A), and giving students steps to follow in writing argumentation provides the structure they need (B). Collaborative writing develops cooperative learning and social skills while teachers set individual within-group performance expectations and structure; students still practice independently (D). Research also shows that student writing performance improves when teachers give explicit instruction in how to plan, revise, and edit their work (C).

16. C: The sentence in choice C is most likely to be a topic sentence of a paragraph, as it contains a transition word used for introducing a final main point (finally), and it introduces the neurological aspects of screen time in order to set up supporting evidence and discussion related to this topic. Choice A is incorrect because this sentence has the force and suggestion of real-life application that is characteristic of concluding paragraphs. Choice B is incorrect because it states that there are negative effects of screen time. This suggests that at least some of these effects will be listed or explained later which is consistent with an introductory paragraph sentence. Choice D is incorrect because it appears to be a supporting detail, given the transition word "also" that places it in a series and the narrow focus of the sentence on developmental delays.

17. A: In both the fictional narrative genre and the nonfictional informational genre, the author will demonstrate some individual writing style; even very factual and objective expositional writing will reveal some personal stylistic characteristics. Labeled diagrams and photos are more likely to be found in informational nonfiction. The majority of books with excitement and drama are fictional narratives (some informational nonfiction books are presented in narrative form and include excitement, especially in children's literature, but these are the minority). Themes and plots are also literary elements associated with fictional narrative.

18. B: Readers should first identify the conclusion of an argument and then identify the premises the author gives to support that conclusion. Choice A is incorrect because the reader cannot find support premises without knowing the conclusion that needs to be supported. Choice C is incorrect because the author may present supporting premises before their argument's conclusion, but readers should first identify the conclusion when evaluating arguments. Choice D is incorrect because readers should try to paraphrase the premises to clarify them and show how they support the conclusion.

19. B: Students should always target an audience, perform an audience analysis, and develop an audience profile to determine what they should include in or omit from their writing. Even though the assigning teacher may be the only one to read the writing, students still need to identify an audience (A) and should not write as if the teacher is the main audience (D). In addition to knowing their purpose for writing before beginning, students should also consider what purpose their writing will meet for their readers (C) and how it is likely to be used.

20. A: Despite its length, this is a simple sentence—one independent clause. The predicate is compound, meaning that one subject has two or more parallel verb phrases. In this case, "the tall man" serves as the subject for *entered*, *walked*, and *sat down*. It is not complex (B), as it has no dependent clause; not compound (C), as it has only one independent clause; and not compound-complex (D), as it has only one independent clause and no dependent clause.

21. A: In the organization stage of writing, the writer determines the purpose, thesis, and supporting details of the written work. In other words, the organization stage is the part of the writing process where the writer decides on the structure of the proposed written work. In this stage, the writer organizes the ideas already decided upon in the prewriting stage.

22. C: The sentences within one effective paragraph should all be related to one another and to one main idea. Unrelated sentences in a paragraph show poor focus, so choice C is correct. Unclear transitions (A) will certainly make a paragraph less effective, but they are not necessarily an example of poor focus, as the ideas may all relate to one main point but simply not be connected well. A paragraph should have only one main idea, so there would be no way to have too few main ideas (B). A lack of solid evidence (D) will make a paragraph less effective, but it is not an example of poor focus.

23. D: The sentence in choice D states a finding objectively, without using language that could be seen as persuasive, grandiose, casual, equivocating, etc., so choice D is correct. The sentence in choice A makes a casual, sweeping generalization by saying *everyone needs*, so choice A is incorrect. The choice B sentence has a grandiose or over-confident mood due to the use of *beyond any doubt*, so choice B is not correct. Choice C has a self-deprecating mood that seems to say, in so many words, that the research was fruitless and the reader has wasted their time, so choice C is incorrect. Even if the research did not go as planned, a conclusion can be made that further research is needed in a particular area.

24. B: Techniques promoting paragraph coherence include transitions (i.e., using words and phrases to connect ideas and sentences), repetition (i.e., repeating key words and phrases across sentences to reinforce their importance as well as help sentences flow together), parallelism (i.e., using adjacent phrases, clauses, or sentences that have the same syntax to make information easier to process), and consistency (i.e., making point of view, tone, register, voice, etc. uniform across a piece of writing). Since repetition is the only one of these that focuses on showing importance, choice B is correct, and the other choices are incorrect.

25. B: Choice B is correct because dialogue can be used to bring themes and meanings into clearer focus and change the course of the plot. Choice A is incorrect because dialogue can be used to advance the plot and to develop characters. Choice C is incorrect because dialogue should not be used merely to break up exposition, and it does not by itself slow the pace of the story. Choice D is incorrect because dialogue can be used to reproduce real-life speech patterns and to add drama to a story.

26. D: The clue for identifying infinitives is the word *to* before a verb. In this case, *to reflect* and *to enlighten* are excellent examples of infinitives, which are a type of verbal, or a verb form that actually function as a different part of speech. Infinitives (and gerunds) function as nouns.

27. A: The first step a reader should take in evaluating the arguments in an informational text is to identify the conclusion the author draws with the argument. The second step is to identify what premises or reasons support this conclusion. The third step is to clarify these premises or reasons by paraphrasing them in the reader's own words, which can also show whether the premises fit with the conclusion they should support. The reader can then list all premises in order, followed by the conclusion, and note any assumptions or premises necessary to support the conclusion that the author may have omitted. The next step is judging whether a deductive reasoning argument is valid, or whether an inductive reasoning argument uses true premises that support the conclusion.

28. B: Authors of informational texts may occasionally explicitly state their point of view, but there are more cases where the author is acting as an expert, a neutral observer, or some other ostensibly objective voice. Therefore, readers will often need to infer the author's point of view. Choice A is incorrect because there is no requirement in informational writing that the author's point of view be part of the main idea. Choice C is incorrect because seeing the author's point of view is generally easier when the author is extreme or opinionated and harder when they seem neutral or balanced. This also means that some analysis is usually required, but the need for analysis does not indicate that the writing is poor, so choice D is incorrect.

29. A: The text at hand contains several clues as to the meaning of this word, including the use of the words "peaceful" and "quiet" in the preceding sentence. Students may also recognize that Mom's requests for help with undesirable household chores interrupted Dad's peaceful, quiet 'reverie." Choice A is the specific method that would be most appropriate for determining the word's meaning; Choice B is a less reliable or systematic way of doing the same thing. Choice C would not be helpful in this case since "reverie" is not a word that can be decoded in a traditional manner. Choice D would not offer a realistic solution to this question since previewing and reviewing are more helpful in increasing comprehension of informative texts, rather than vocabulary words.

30. B, C: There is no inconsistency of verb tense in this sentence, nor is there any misplaced modifier; however, "To better serve you" is a split infinitive, which is a controversial construction in English even if not always considered ungrammatical. The second comma creates a comma splice (i.e., incorrectly separating two independent clauses with a comma instead of the correct punctuation).

31. D: Charles Dickens uses a series of opposites to convey the idea that the period described involves extremes of positive and negative. He also likens the period to the present time in that certain institutions are interested in people believing in these extremes. He does not say that the extremes are only imagined (A), that personal subjectivity dictates whether a given extreme is seen as good or bad (B), or that this past era and the present era are identical (C).

32. A: The even rhythm and ample use of anaphora emphasize the concept of equal, opposing forces. Anaphora is the repetition of a phrase to start consecutive clauses, creating a parallel. The presentation of multiple opposites introduces a theme of doubles that highlights conflict rather than contradiction, so choice B is not correct. Choice C is not correct because it mentions anastrophe, which reverses adjective-noun order to noun-adjective, such as in the phrase "ocean blue." Anaphora is relevant here, not anastrophe. Repetition of an entire sentence can be used to slow the pacing in a story, but the repetition here is limited to the beginnings of the clauses. The ending of each clause is different, so there is no slowing effect, making choice D incorrect.

33. C: In the sense that Charles Dickens uses them here, *light* and *darkness* do not mean physical illumination or its absence. Their meanings are instead figurative, with *light* referring to good, knowledge, happiness, hope, etc., and *darkness* referring to bad, ignorance, unhappiness, despair, etc. The other three choices all use words whose most literal meaning is applicable, so these pairs are not figurative in meaning.

34. A: Because of the balancing of opposites in the introduction, readers can infer that this balance will likely be present throughout the story. There is no reason to expect it will focus more on bad, as choice B states. Though the introduction mentions that the "superlative degree of comparison" is "for good or for evil," it does not suggest that there is really no difference between good and bad, so choice C is incorrect. Choice D is incorrect because, even though the story may show how good can come from bad, there is no reason to view this possibility as particularly likely from reading the passage.

35. B: To evaluate articles, readers should consider whether the publishing journals include advertising, and if so, what the advertising is for, as this can influence the content, so (B) is correct. To evaluate books, readers should consider whether any historical perspectives are applicable, so (A) is incorrect. Furthermore, (C) is incorrect because we cannot assume that information in books is out of date. Rather, determining whether the information is out of date is particularly important with books, since books vary widely in terms of currency of information. Finding and reading book reviews can inform evaluations of books, so (D) is incorrect.

36. A: An effective way to teach students the difference between denotation and connotation is to provide example sentences and have students choose a given word that best expresses the connotation of a highlighted word in each sentence. For example, to show the connotation of the word *challenge*, an example sentence "This is one of the many challenges that must be faced in order to solve the problem" could be given, and students could choose whether the connotation suggested by "challenges" in this case was "threats," "obstacles," "criticisms," or "setbacks." This instructional strategy is summarized in choice A, which is the correct answer. Since words generally have denotations and may or may not have connotations depending on their use, a Venn diagram would be misleading, and choice B is incorrect. Choice C is also incorrect, as highlighting words in a passage would not require students to distinguish between denotations and connotations, nor even to identify the exact connotations of words in context. Choice D would not be logical, since not all words have an emotional connotation, and the definition alone will be of little use for determining the connotations of a specific use of a word.

37. D: Kate Chopin narrates some of the events in this story in a different order than they actually occur chronologically, and this makes the end more surprising to readers. She also omits some details. For example, there is no mention of Brently's trip home until he arrives, so readers are just as surprised as Louise is to see him (B). Chopin does NOT omit all description of Louise; she not only lets her actions speak (C) for her in many instances, but also uses description of her appearance and behavior to inform her character.

38. C: Authors who normally write informational text will often need to develop proposals that communicate the value of projects to those unfamiliar with the technicalities, so choice C is the correct answer. Moreover, they may need to communicate simpler, clearer messages rather than dense content, meaning choice A is incorrect. Professionals in relevant fields would likely be familiar enough with the subject matter to understand technical language, while experts in the subject are unlikely to need nontechnical explanations at all, making choices B and D incorrect.

39. C: The goal of a persuasive essay is to convince the reader that the author's position or opinion on a topic is correct. That opinion or position is called the argument. A persuasive essay argues a series of points that are supported by facts and evidence.

40. A: This is a simple sentence, which is a single independent clause (containing a compound verb). Choice B is a complex sentence, which has a dependent clause ("Although you can run") that could not be a sentence on its own and depends on the independent clause ("you can't hide"), which could be a sentence by itself. Choice C is a compound sentence, which has two independent clauses joined by the coordinating conjunction *but*. Choice D is a compound–complex sentence that includes two independent clauses separated by a semicolon ("Run; run fast"), each of which could be stand-alone sentences, and a dependent clause ("because you can't hide"), which could not.

41. C: In MLA format, books include the publisher's name, and periodical articles include the periodical title and, when available, the volume number, issue number, and page numbers, regardless of whether the source is print or electronic. Choice A is incomplete because it addresses only books, and choice B is incomplete because it addresses only periodical articles. Choice D is incorrect because database information and URLs apply only to certain electronic sources and are not the source-specific details required for all sources.

42. B: One criterion for evaluating source credibility is whether or not the text underwent peer review, which is a process by which experts in a field review a work to determine its suitability for publication. While the peer review process has its downsides, one can rely on a journal article that has been peer reviewed to be a credible source for academic research. Choice A is incorrect because a text can be cited even if it contains outdated information, so long as the information being used is not outdated itself. Also note that outdated information is not merely old information, but information that has been found to be inaccurate by later research; therefore, older research may contain many elements that are outdated but still include accurate and relevant information useful for citation. Choice C is incorrect because the value and relevance of a text should be judged by consulting other related sources as well as other texts that have cited the text as a source. Choice D is incorrect because public awareness of or familiarity with an organization does not ensure that the texts the organization has published are credible from an academic standpoint.

43. C: Choice C is correct. The author of the poem asks "what immortal hand or eye,/Could frame" the tiger's "fearful symmetry." In these two lines, "immortal" suggests the idea of a creator god, and "frame" refers to creating not just the physical animal but the concept of the animal. Choice A is incorrect, though the tiger's ferociousness is the subject of awe expressed in the poem. Choice B is incorrect, as the poem does not ask why the tiger seems fearsome but does present some imagery that conveys the fearsomeness of the tiger. Choice D is incorrect; while the poem refers to the origins of the tiger (specifically "the fire of [the tiger's] eyes"), it does not ask by what process these traits developed or came to be feared.

44. B: The first part of the introduction to an essay or paper should be a sentence or series of sentences that will get the reader's attention so that they are interested in continuing to read. Such a sentence or series of sentences may be called an "attention-getter" or "hook," so choice B is correct. Following the hook should be some pertinent background information followed by the thesis statement, which is a clear expression of the main point the writer is trying to make in the essay or paper. Since the thesis statement does not come first, choice A is incorrect. An optional part of the introduction is an explanation of how the thesis will be supported or defended that highlights the main points to follow in the body paragraphs. As this is usually at the end of the introduction, choice D is incorrect. Another optional part of the introduction is a portion that informs the reader of the writer's reason for choosing the essay or paper's specific topic. The most appropriate place for this explanation would be between the hook and the thesis, so choice C is incorrect.

45. C: Realist authors strive to represent reality as closely as possible, even in fiction. They avoid exaggeration, which satire often employs to ridicule social behaviors. Though irony is particularly key in satire, realists often use it as well, such as in O. Henry's "The Gift of the Magi," so choice A is not correct. Both genres may involve writing in a serious tone, ruling out choice B. Jonathan Swift intensifies the satirical effects of "A Modest Proposal" by making absurd and even horrific recommendations in an ostensibly serious tone. Finally, choice D is not correct because vernacular dialogue is used in both genres, though generally for different purposes.

46. C: In a paired reading activity to practice identifying main ideas and details (thereby improving informational text reading comprehension), both students read the same piece of text silently, so choice C is correct. The purpose of the exercise is to have both students gather all they can from the text themselves and then compare what they found. They do not read aloud taking turns (A) or simultaneously (B), and they do not read separate pieces of the same text (D).

47. A: Bloggers need to use correct punctuation to encourage continued reading of their posts. If they are not already confident in their grasp of punctuation, they should write in shorter sentences until they are. Because reading on computer screens is harder than on paper, paragraphs in blogs must be significantly shorter than in print, not longer. Shorter paragraphs enable readers to "chunk" the information. Font sizes should be larger rather than smaller to be easier on readers' eyes and more legible onscreen.

48. A: While there is no consensus among experts as to any universal sequence of instruction for teaching the alphabetic principle through phonics instruction, they do agree that, to enable children to start reading words as soon as possible, the highest-utility relationships should be introduced earliest. For example, the letters *m, a, p, t,* and *s* are all used frequently, whereas the *x* in *box*, the sound of *ey* in *they*, and the letter *a* when pronounced as it is in *want* have lower-utility letter-sound correspondences. Important considerations for the alphabetic principle are to teach letter-sound correspondences in isolation, not in word contexts; to teach them explicitly; to give students opportunities to practice letter-sound relationships within their other daily lessons, not only separately; and to include cumulative reviews of relationships taught earlier along with new ones in practice opportunities.

49. D: First the writer should narrow down all potential topics to a main idea. Then he or she should identify main points supporting that main idea, decide how to sequence those main points (B), list all the details that support each of the main points (A), and then organize those details in a logical, effective order (C).

50. A: The poem from which this excerpt is taken is Walt Whitman's celebration of a mystical experience revealing, among other themes, his unity with the universe and nature. This oneness, though it seems to come through death, is spoken about in terms of willingness and welcome in the phrases "I bequeath myself" and "the grass I love." Therefore, choice A is correct. Choice B is incorrect because these lines do not imply the poet's view of his social class. Whitman's use of the phrase "under your boot-soles" literally refers to the ground rather than figuratively referring to perceived social inferiority. Choice C is incorrect because the persona seems casual and even lighthearted about dying, as in the phrase "look for me under your boot-soles." Choice D is incorrect, as these lines give no evidence of emotional harm to the persona, but only a mention of where the audience or listener can look "if you want me again."

51. A: This sentence is an analogy, which compares two concepts to establish a relationship, so choice A is correct. Analogy can enhance comprehension of a new concept via comparison to an older or more familiar concept. Allegory (B) uses symbolism to represent an abstract concept with a more concrete concept. Allusion (C) is a passing reference to a specific work, place, person, or event. For example, saying "Susan loves to help and care for other people so much that her friends call her Mother Teresa" is an allusion to a famous person that makes a point about how compassionate someone is. Antithesis (D) juxtaposes words, phrases, or sentences with opposite meanings, balancing these to add insight. A good example is Neil Armstrong's statement during the moon landing: "That's one small step for man, one giant leap for mankind."

52. B: Teachers should base rubrics on their identified lesson objectives. They should explain a rubric to students in advance, and have students refer to the rubric as a guide while they work. Teachers should then use the rubric to assess whether students have met all included learning objectives. Rubrics can be used as both formative and summative assessment tools, meaning they were assessed either during or after the work, respectively. Rubrics are not replacements for clearly stating learning goals, objectives, expectations, and teacher modeling of expected performance: teachers should do all of these to enable optimal student performance, as well as supply a rubric to guide and assess student work. Teachers should also make very clear to students the relationship between learning goals and their performance.

53. C: William Shakespeare's plays are good literary examples of poetry within fictional drama because they are written in verse form. Poems typically do not contain inserted prose (A). Plays are not generally known to incorporate pieces of fictional prose (B). Nonfictional prose sometimes incorporates quotations of poetry or even occasionally original poems, but this occurs much less often than with Shakespeare's plays and many others written entirely or mostly in poetry (D).

54. C: This is an example of a dangling participle. The participle *completing* was done by Peter, but the sentence construction makes it seem as if the teacher did it. This makes no sense: the teacher would not give Peter a high grade after completing the assignment correctly. It can be corrected to "After Peter completed the assignment correctly, the teacher gave him a high grade" or "After completing the assignment correctly, Peter received a high grade from the teacher."

55. B: Quoting other writers is a good technique for incorporating outside sources into a research paper, but students are advised to keep quotations brief. Longer quotations (c)—e.g., 6–8 long excerpts within a 10-page paper—are excessive. Students sometimes do this to pad their paper length, but they end up with more of others' material than their own. Students should also avoid ending their papers with quotations (a). This can be a ploy to prevent readers from challenging their assertions, to avoid thinking critically and considering multiple alternatives regarding the topic, and/or to avoid writing anything more in their own words about it. Quotations are better used to generate discussion than to suppress it. Students should also quote sources that both support and refute their assertions, not only the former (d). Readers with normal skepticism can more readily agree with writers' positions when they present evidence on both sides of an issue.

56. C: The part of speech that identifies a person, place, or thing is a noun (A). The part of speech that describes an action or state of being is a verb (B). The part of speech that describes a noun, tells how many of a noun there are, or specifies one noun as distinct from another noun is an adjective (D). An adverb is the part of speech that modifies (or describes) a verb, adjective, or adverb, making choice C correct.

57. D: Collaborative Strategic Reading (CSR) is a technique that largely depends on cooperative learning and practice of metacognition. In practice, this look slike putting students into groups and having them self-monitor their own reading comprehension using various reading strategies. One popular reading strategy that can be used includes "click and clunk," which is where students report which parts of the story *click* to them, or which makes sense without much difficulty, and which parts *clunk*, or are not easy to understand. Then the group would collaborate to resolve the clunks and ensure everyone understood the reading assignment. Other strategies can include use of context clues, rereading, or any other reading comprehension strategy, paired with group discussion.

58. A: A verb forms or starts the predicate of a sentence, so choice A is correct. As an example, in *She went to the store*, *went* is the verb and *to the store* is a prepositional phrase modifying the verb. Together, these form the predicate. The other answer choices refer to parts of speech that may be included in the predicate, but are not essential to forming a predicate, like verbs are. A noun can be the subject of a sentence or an object in a sentence. In the preceding example, the pronoun *she* is the subject, while the noun *store* is the object of a preposition. An adjective modifies (i.e., gives more information about) a noun or another adjective. An adverb modifies a verb, an adjective, or another adverb.

59. A: This describes the poetic form of haiku, which originated in Japanese poetic tradition and has been adopted by other languages. Though Japanese haiku can be translated for meaning, doing so generally necessitates different numbers of syllables. American poet Ezra Pound's 1911 poem "In a Station of the Metro" is sometimes viewed as an early example of haiku being adopted in English. The poem reads:

> *The apparition of these faces in the crowd:*
> *Petals on a wet, black bough.*

Sonnets, limericks, and cinquains are all poetic forms with well-defined structures, but they have their own rules for meter and do not follow the five-seven-five syllabification of haiku.

60. A: The narrator never admits insanity. From the beginning of the story on, he unequivocally denies it numerous times. This is one of the ways that Poe shows that the narrator is indeed insane. Another is by using the narrator to speak about the murder in a matter-of-fact manner that is sometimes excitedly proud, showing a casual lack of remorse that would be uncharacteristic of a sane person who commits a murder and then must confront the gravity of his or her crime and its consequences (B). Poe also develops the theme through the narrator's obsession with the victim's "Evil Eye" (C). Furthermore, the narrator seems to the reader to be delusional because the narrator imagines sounds or mistakes certain sounds for other sounds, all the while believing that a medical condition has given them heightened senses (D).

61. C: In news writing, important information generally comes first, as this serves the main purpose of news by providing key information before the reader decides to move on to another story. Choice A is not correct because essays are not restricted to persuasion and the main purpose of news is not to entertain. Choice B is not correct because news articles can have a formal tone, and both essays and news articles should sound objective. Choice D is not correct because, while essays tend to relate to academic topics and news articles to current events, neither is restricted to these areas.

62. C: The author is hoping to persuade or convince readers to either request a pet and/or the primary care of their pet by providing them with facts as well as by using rhetorical devices such as dispelling opposing arguments.

63. A: "In kitchen cups concupiscent curds" makes use of alliteration, the repetition of the same initial consonant sound (in this case, the sound /k/) in consecutive words, or in words in the same phrase. Hyperbole (B) is the device of exaggeration. Onomatopoeia (C) is the device of words sounding like what they mean. For example, in "the clang of the bell," the pronunciation of the word *clang* sounds like the noise the bell is making. Metonymy (D) is the device of referring to a noun by an associated thing, such as using "the White House" to mean the U.S. government or using "Hollywood" to mean the American film industry.

64. D: Critics understand "The Emperor of Ice-Cream" to have been written about a wake, and Wallace Stevens is drawing a contrast between the festive atmosphere at the wake and the reality that a person has died. Though these contrasts may lead to different interpretations from different readers, line 7 fits into the contrast by telling readers to let the way things truly are be the "finale" of the way things seem—to let *seem* build up to the reality of *be*. The sentence in Choice D summarizes this best, so it is the correct answer. Choice A is a possible interpretation of the poem as a whole, but it does not match with the progression in line 7 from seeming to being, but rather from being to accepting. Choice B connects with the ostensibly festive atmosphere and the reality of death that is the backdrop, but it also does not match line 7 in that it suggests seeming is better than being. Choice C arguably matches the progression in line 7 from seeming to being with good to bad, but line 7 does not explicitly say that seeming is good and being is bad, or that seeming should be appreciated.

65. B: The first sentence has a clear meaning based on syntax, but the second sentence is slightly ambiguous.

In sentence 1, *with a broken arm* modifies *the man*, so it is the man that has a broken arm, and the man sat in a chair. The man is the subject of the sentence and the adjective "with a broken arm" immediately follows and can only be interpreted one way.

In English, adjectives are typically placed close to the noun that they modify, so most readers would assume the adjectival phrase "with a broken arm" found in sentence 2 modifies the word *chair* and not *the man.* Despite this common usage, English allows for syntactic variation and leaves sentence 2 technically unclear. The following modified sentences help to demonstrate how an adjective in this sentence structure can modify either the subject (*the man*) or the object (*a chair*).

	subject: "The man"; object: "a chair"; adjectival phrase: "with a broken arm"
Unclear adjective placement:	"The man sat in a chair with a broken arm."
Adjective modifiying the subject:	"The man sat on a *pillow* with a broken arm."
Adjective modifiying the object:	"The man sat on a chair with a broken *wheel*."

In these cases, context can help inform and clarify meaning when the syntax is not clear enough to determine which noun is being modified.

66. B: The age norms for correctly pronouncing these most difficult of phonemes, /r/ and /s/, are around seven to eight years old. Thus a four-year-old who substitutes /w/ for /r/, lisps on /s/ or otherwise distorts it, or omits either/both of these sounds likely has normal development in speech articulation. Delayed language development (A) is not signaled by mispronouncing phonemes but by being significantly behind age norms for comprehending and constructing language. Hearing impairment (C) often causes misarticulations; however, errors in only two difficult phonemes when far below the age norms do not indicate it. Misarticulating phonemes is not a symptom of stuttering (D).

67. C: Screening assessments are given to identify students who may be at future risk of academic difficulties and may benefit from interventions. Diagnostic assessments can then be given to confirm or provide additional information about screening results, including identifying students' specific strengths and needs. This information can then be used to guide instruction.

68. B: Research studies have shown that teaching self-regulation helps students become aware of their own strengths and weaknesses in writing, so choice B is correct. Choice A is incorrect because teaching self-regulation has been shown to make writing efforts more strategic, better targeting desired results. Choice C is incorrect because teaching self-regulation has been shown to help students inhibit their emotions, thoughts, and behaviors when this is necessary. Choice D is incorrect because teaching self-regulation encourages self-management and empowers students to adapt writing strategies as needed.

69. A: The introduction of an essay should get the reader's attention, engage the reader's interest, state and integrate the main thesis within it, and give an overview of the essay's organization or structure (for example, by summarizing the main point and supporting evidence). Developing the thesis statement and giving examples of the idea in the thesis both belong in the body of the essay. Giving the reader a sense of closure belongs in the conclusion of the essay.

70. B: Drawing inferences in an informational text helps readers understand ideas that are not explicitly stated in the text, so choice B is correct. Choice A is incorrect because drawing inferences is not critical in recalling specific details from thuee text. On the contrary, one could recall all of the explicit details from the text without making any inferences. Choice C is incorrect because inferences can be made and often are made based upon only a portion of the text. The information necessary to make inferences is not what the whole text says, but what part of the text says combined with what the reader already knows. Choice D is incorrect because readers have no need to articulate questions about the text in order to make inferences. Making inferences is indeed helpful in answering questions the reader has about the text, but these questions do not need to be articulated.

71. C: Full reading comprehension of informational text depends on both the reader's ability to recall information or prior knowledge and the reader's ability to make inferences based on that information and the text. Therefore, choice C is correct, and choices A, B, and D are incorrect.

72. B: Personification is the attributing of human qualities to something not human. Here, the landscape listens and shadows hold their breath, mimicking human or animal behavior. Assonance is the repetition of vowel sounds, which is not evident here, making choice A wrong. A simile is a comparison of two unlike things using the words *like* or *as*. Because that is not the case here, choice C is incorrect. A metaphor is a direct comparison, which is not the case in these lines, making choice D wrong.

73. B: **Split infinitive.** Correction: "to shout your answers loudly."

74. A: The sentence in choice A uses two metaphors: "He became a tiger" and "he turned into a pussycat." These give readers a better understanding of the person being discussed by comparing his qualities, characteristics, and behaviors to those of more familiar examples—in this case, tigers and domestic cats. Metaphors explicitly state one thing is another, while similes use "like" or "as" to make comparisons. Although similes are also considered figurative language, they are not metaphors, making choice B incorrect. Choices C and D are incorrect because both of these sentences are literal.

75. A: Introducing new vocabulary words will help students decode the words faster when they are encountered in the text, thus assisting with fluency. Recognizing the words and knowing their meanings will also build readers' confidence. Additionally, explaining the meanings of the words in advance will help students comprehend the text when they read it independently. Reading the first few pages aloud without discussion will not help students recognize or understand the vocabulary words, nor will it highlight important words beyond the first few pages. Listing what students want to learn about the topic helps to set a purpose for reading, not explain vocabulary. Predicting helps students activate prior knowledge, make connections, and stay actively engaged in the reading process.

76. C: When students write for their classmates, they should use language that is more informal and age-appropriate, not more sophisticated (A). Jargon also gives the general impression of confusing language where simpler language would be effective. When describing a procedure to a colleague, especially one who is considered an expert, a writer should not need to use simple language (B), as the colleague will likely understand relevant technical or sophisticated language. When writing for younger children, students should use more vivid and entertaining language (C), including some humor when appropriate. When asking parental permission for more independent activities, students should use language that seems more mature and serious rather than using humor (D).

77. C: Choice C is correct, since the verbs mentioned in the question all refer to interpreting information in one's own words—which involves the cognitive objective of comprehension. Tasks targeting knowledge recall (A) would ask students to name, label, list, define, repeat, memorize, order, or arrange material. Tasks targeting application (B) would ask students to calculate, solve, practice, operate, sketch, use, prepare, illustrate, or apply material. Tasks targeting evaluation (D) would ask students to judge, appraise, evaluate, conclude, predict, score, or compare material.

78. A: Although pausing before answering a question can extend the length of a speaker's presentation, it does not affect the conciseness of their speech. In fact, speakers should not avoid or fear pausing before answering questions. Pausing before answering a question allows time to formulate an answer and shows that the speaker is taking the time to give a thoughtful answer. Choice B is incorrect because inclusion of unnecessary details decreases conciseness. If a speaker prioritizes interesting details over necessary ones, they are likely to produce a speech that meanders and is not concise. Although the inclusion of details and personal anecdotes can sometimes help with audience engagement, choice C is incorrect because the inclusion of too many details and anecdotes can take away from the main topic and decrease the overall level of conciseness. When evaluating the conciseness of a speech, it is important to evaluate these anecdotes and details to make sure their inclusion is necessary to help the speaker make their point. If these details do not help with this purpose, the speech is unlikely to be concise. Choice D is incorrect because, while the time needed to answer a question or cover a point varies depending on the topic and the audience of the speech, the speaker can still spend an inappropriate amount of time on a particular point.

79. B: By observing sentence syntax (i.e., structure, word order, word endings, etc.), a reader can nearly always determine an unfamiliar word's part of speech (e.g., a noun, verb, adjective, or adverb). Therefore, choice B is correct. The other choices either state that syntax nearly always reveal's a word's meaning (choice A). Both meaning and part of speech (choice C), or neither meaning nor part of speech (choice D), and are therefore incorrect.

80. A: A primary characteristic of informative or explanatory writing is that the author assumes certain facts or truths, as informative writing is an attempt to work from existing knowledge in order to convey new knowledge. Therefore, choice A is correct. Choice B is incorrect because descriptive writing does not rely as heavily on assumed truths. Instead, descriptive writing uses sensory details to allow readers to experience what is being described. Choice C is incorrect because persuasive writing endeavors to convince readers of a truth. Choice D is incorrect because narrative writing relates a story to readers and does not depend on facts.

81. A: Among instructional strategies defined by a master teacher (Robb, 2002), asking students open-ended questions about the texts they read is the most useful for helping students to read critically. Teaching students how to skim text for headings, subheadings, boldface, illustrations, captions, sidebars, the index, and other text features that give signs (B) of pertinent material is most useful for helping students locate information. Guiding students to make connections between text and their own personal experiences (D), everyday life (C), world events, and other texts is most useful for helping students understand the relevance of learning materials.

82. A: Audience members are most likely to retain the points of a speech or lecture if they are offered in the form of a story and the speaker uses language that is simple and direct enough to be transparent. The stories need to be simple, and must drive the speech directly toward an essential and clear point. Including anecdotes is most effective when the speaker uses storytelling techniques that will bring them alive, such as varying pace, pitch, and intensity, using body language to suggest a change in speakers, and using the stage to suggest a setting.

83. C: Adjective/adverb confusion. *Quick* is an adjective that can modify a noun ("a quick trip") or another adjective. The adverb *quickly* would modify the verb *give.*

84. B: The paragraph structural pattern of narration (A) tells readers a story or part of one. The structural pattern of description (B) shows readers instead of telling them. The classification (C) pattern groups individual objects, beings, or ideas into categories by similarity, commonality, or according to an inclusive principle. The pattern of giving examples (D) illustrates points or ideas instead of telling, showing, or grouping them.

85. B: Shakespeare (1564-1616) wrote during the Renaissance (B), which is generally considered to encompass the 15th and 16th centuries. The medieval (A) era, also known as the Middle Ages, was earlier, ending in the late 15th century, and included authors like Geoffrey Chaucer, Dante Alighieri, the author of *Sir Gawain and the Green Knight,* and Sir Thomas Malory. The Restoration (C) period in English literature followed the Renaissance, starting in the middle of the 17th century and ending before the 18th century. It included authors like John Dryden, who wrote poetry, satire, and criticism. The Enlightenment (D) occurred in the 18th century and included the authors Jonathan Swift, Alexander Pope, Dr. Samuel Johnson, and James Boswell.

86. B: When an informational text author does not explicitly state their point of view or purpose, the reader should determine this themselves by asking certain questions. Evaluating the effectiveness of the author's choice and use of evidence is not helpful for determining author point of view or purpose, so choice B is correct. There are four considerations the reader can make in order to determine the author's point of view or purpose: what the author wants to accomplish by writing the text (A), what the author wants to persuade readers to agree with or believe (C), how the author's word choice affects the reader's perceptions of the subject matter (D), and how the author's choices of examples or facts affect the reader's perceptions of the subject matter.

87. D: This is a simple sentence despite its length. It has only one independent clause, which contains a single subject (He) and a compound predicate with multiple verbs (woke, looked, got, ate, got, drove, parked, walked, opened, went). All other parts are prepositions, prepositional phrases, adjectives, adverbs, and articles modifying verbs and nouns. The other types all include more than one clause—either more than one independent plus at least one dependent clause (A), more than one independent clause (B), or an independent and a dependent clause (C).

88. A: In this sentence, the word *trouvère* functions as the object of the preposition, which can be either a noun or a pronoun Because pronoun is not an option, the only choice is noun.

89. C: Choice C is correct because journaling can be a form of free writing, which serves to develop writing skills. Choice A is incorrect as many journals are written for documentation or autobiographical purposes, and many authors write journals they expect or hope to publish someday. Choice B is incorrect because journals are not confined to any particular form or structure. Choice D is incorrect because journaling is often used for its therapeutic benefits for the writer.

90. B: Both authors use the first-person omniscient narrator in these novels. In *The Lovely Bones*, a girl who has died can observe her living family and provides omniscient narration. In *The Book Thief*, the first-person omniscient narrator is Death, who tells the story of the main character, Liesel, interspersed with his own thoughts and feelings. First-person narrators appear as a character in the story and refer to themselves using first-person pronouns. Both novels are written in first-person, but they are not limited to the perspective, thoughts, or experiences of the narrator, making choice B correct and choice C incorrect. Third-person narrators do not exist as a character with their own thoughts, feelings, and motivations. Instead, they are an outside observer relaying what is happening to the reader. Third-person omniscient narrators refer to characters in the third person and know the characters' inner thoughts, feelings, and motivations. Narrators using third-person limited narration, choice D, tell the story from the perspective of one character, but will refer to the character by name or a third-person pronoun. This type of narrator typically only makes the reader aware of one character's thoughts, feelings, and perspectives, while third-person omniscient narrators may refer to the inner thoughts of multiple characters.

91. B: Split infinitive. "He found it easier <u>to complete</u> the form more efficiently online."

92. B: Imagery is description that activates readers' senses so they can more clearly imagine what is described. For example, in the poem *The Waste Land,* T. S. Eliot conveys a civilization's decay through images of dried-up wells, crumbling towers, and toppled tombstones. A simile is an explicit comparison using *like* or *as*, such as William Wordsworth's famous line "I wandered lonely as a cloud." A metaphor is an implicit comparison. In a metaphor, the writer equates one thing to another. The reader is expected to understand that it is a comparison and not to be taken literally. Hyperbole deliberately exaggerates for effect, as in Mark Twain's line "I ... could have hung my hat on my eyes, they stuck out so far." Although simile, metaphors, and hyperbole can be used in imagery, they do not always use description to activate the reader's senses, such as in the metaphor "time is money."

93. D: Teachers can best employ strategic demands on children who are learning new vocabulary by beginning at a low level of demand and moving to high-demand questions. This effectively scaffolds new instruction by building up from simple and easy to complex and difficult. Alternation can be helpful as well, but instructing at a high level early on may result in confusion and frustration, rather than an improved grasp of a concept. (B) describes a constructivist approach to vocabulary, which can work for more abstract concepts. As students naturally encounter a concept, they build their own understanding of how something works. This approach may not be the best method for vocabulary acquisition, as students may arrive at inaccurate meanings. Similarly, (C) suggests keeping the rigor low until students have mastery over the new vocabulary, but vocabulary requires understanding terms in shallow and in deep ways and requires interaction with the word in a variety of applications to truly master a concept. Oversimplification can lead to inaccurate knowledge and possibly even frustration. Instead, a teacher should begin with a clear and simple definition and work toward complex applications as students are capable.

94. C: While researching a topic and related vocabulary can help a reader make a better evaluation, this action does not require the reader to evaluate the methods of appeal used in a text. The other choices refer to actions that require some form of evaluation on the part of the reader. These include paraphrasing, summarizing, or outlining the text using their own words (A); considering the effectiveness of other methods of appeal (B); and considering the types of appeals the author uses and why (D).

95. C: Good essay organization has many benefits. First, good organization makes the reader more likely to accept the validity of the writer's thesis, making choice A incorrect. Good organization also helps to keep the reader's attention, so choice B is incorrect. Since well-organized essays typically follow a standard format, identifying main ideas is usually easier for readers, which makes choice D incorrect. Choice C is correct because good organization requires more effort from the writer, but it results in easier understanding for the reader.

96. D: Choice D is correct because it contains phrases that are used to indicate the presence of an additional supporting detail. These phrases are generally used to introduce a new supporting detail that is related to the previous supporting detail (e.g., Penguins have many feathers that help keep them warm. Additionally, their feathers help to wick away water). Choice A is incorrect because these phrases are used to show contrast between two or more ideas (e.g., Although penguins are flightless birds, they are fast swimmers). Choice B is incorrect because these phrases are best for drawing attention to an idea or providing a "fun fact" that supports or reinforces the idea (e.g., Many species of penguins mate for life. In fact, male Adelie and Gentoo penguins "propose" to their mate using smooth pebbles). Choice C is incorrect because these phrases are used to indicate that an example is about to be provided (e.g. Penguins eat many sea creatures, such as krill and fish).

97. D: A simple (A) sentence has only a single independent clause. A complex (B) sentence has at least one independent and one dependent clause. A compound (C) sentence has at least two independent clauses, but no dependent clauses. A compound–complex (D) sentence has at least two independent clauses, plus at least one dependent clause.

98. C: Throughout this epic poem, Henry Wadsworth Longfellow employs trochaic tetrameter (a trochee is /∪, i.e., two syllables, the first stressed, the second unstressed; tetrameter is four beats per line) to evoke for his readers the rhythms of the Native Americans' chanting. Though he asks and answers a series of questions in his Introduction, Longfellow never uses couplets (A), (B); the stanzas vary in length, but are all longer than two lines each. He does not use irony to develop a theme (D).

99. A: The student making this observation is connecting a reading about mythological gods to the world—in this instance, to human nature—by noting that despite greater powers, the gods' emotional reactions and behaviors are like those of humans. Since this is an example of connecting text to what the student knows about the world choice A is correct. The student statements in choices B and D reflect connections of text to text—fiction (a novel) to historical accounts of a period, and a character description to another story with a similar character. The student statement in option C reflects a connection of text to self; the student can relate to the feelings of a character in the text.

100. B: This is an example of a metaphor. The literal meaning of hemorrhaging is copious bleeding. In this example it is used figuratively in a metaphor for losing money at a volume and rate comparable to severe blood loss denoted by hemorrhage. It is not a generalization. An example of using a generalization persuasively is "We all want peace, not war." It is not a rhetorical question or a question at all. An example of using a rhetorical question (needing no answer) persuasively is "Wouldn't you rather get paid more than less?" The example is not of negative connotation, because the word "hemorrhage" already has a negative denotation—in other words, the literal meaning of hemorrhaging is never a good thing. An example of using negative word connotation persuasively is, "You could stay with this *expensive* plan..." followed by contrasting positive connotation: "...or choose the *money-saving* plan I'm offering."

101. C: The student should consult a grammar guide to determine whether written sentences are complete and correct. An encyclopedia (A) gives comprehensive information on various content subjects and may include grammatical topics, but it will not explicitly define or explain all rules of syntax and grammar. A dictionary (B) gives the correct spellings, pronunciations, parts of speech, meanings, and origins of vocabulary words rather than grammatical rules. The grammar-check feature of a word-processor program (D) is a poor choice because its information is incomplete, it lacks human understanding, its "corrections" are sometimes inaccurate, and it does not systematically explain grammar rules the way a grammar guide does. Moreover, the student would have to type sentences into the word processor for feedback, but he or she could not use it to look up grammar rules.

102. B: Choice B is correct, as natural communication is generally ideal in public speaking, and verbal and nonverbal communication alike should be natural. Choice A is incorrect because speakers should practice their speeches extensively to ensure confidence and ease of delivery; they will not be received as spontaneous in a good way if they stumble, search for words, or stop to consult notes. Choice C is incorrect because the use of humor can be used to engage with the audience and keep their attention. Although too much humor could be distracting, it is a good tool for audience engagement when used appropriately. Choice D is incorrect because random or irrelevant movements (such as hair-twirling, foot-tapping, pencil-tapping, face-rubbing, etc.) will distract the audience rather than engage them.

103. B: The word *first* shows that this sentence describes the beginning of Maria's family's process for planning holiday celebrations. This is an appropriate detail to follow Maria's introductory sentence. Choices A and C are not clearly relevant to the topic sentence. While these may be important details later, neither of these sentences should follow the topic sentence. Choice D should be included later in the composition, as the word *afterwards* shows that the described step occurs later.

104. B: Students are expected to have a variety of skills with respect to viewing, representing, and analyzing visual/media images by the time they enter high school. They should be able to understand visual imagery and how it affects or creates meaning. Students must also learn to deconstruct the messages they see and create their own for the purposes of communicating their own ideas. Choice A would, perhaps, be the goal of a consumerism or economics class, but is not the best choice for this scenario. This game would create understanding in students about different types of visual images, but they are not likely to be the same images used in their schoolwork at this juncture. Choice D is certainly true; the children will likely enjoy the game. However, Choice B most closely matches the educational requirements and standards laid out for students of this age.

105. A: When conducting a literature review, having too many references indicates the research question is too broad and needs narrowing, so choice A is correct. Having too few references indicates the area of investigation or the research question is too narrow and needs broadening, so choice B is incorrect. Having zero references, especially on cutting-edge topics, does not necessarily invalidate the topic or question, so choice C is incorrect. Choice D is incorrect because determining the topic of the research paper should be done prior to searching for references. This will help the writer determine which references are relevant and write a more focused paper.

106. B: The *roman à clef,* or "novel with a key," tells a story that readers cannot fully understand without the "key," which explains some elements and details. The purpose is to disguise truths that are too threatening to state explicitly, so choice B is correct. Choice A is incorrect because the purpose is not to challenge readers, and choice C is incorrect because the purpose is not to deliberately confuse readers; both of these purposes run contrary to one of the main motivations of writing in the first place—to communicate. Writing of painful personal experiences (even in disguise) can give authors catharsis, but the purpose of the *roman à clef* is not to create distance between these experiences and the reader, but to express these disturbing realities without inflicting the same trauma on the reader, so choice D is incorrect.

107. D: A speech differs from an essay in that it is spoken or read aloud to a live audience, where as an essay is published. Because speeches are given at live events, certain components may need to be included that would not be necessary or appropriate in an essay. These components include greetings (to the audience and possibly to honored guests) and thanks (perhaps to the audience for listening or perhaps to those who have helped or influenced the speaker). Therefore, choice D is correct. Choice A is incorrect because speech introductions differ from essay introductions in that they may include some of the elements above. Choice B is incorrect because the body of a speech and the body of an essay should elaborate and provide supporting evidence in a similar fashion. Choice C is incorrect because speech conclusions, while they sometimes need to include information that essay conclusions do not, must be appropriately forceful and engaging, just as essay conclusions should be.

108. A: When a person argues against a proposition on the grounds that it will lead to a chain of similar events that will have an undesirable outcome, they are using the slippery slope fallacy. In the example given, the person opposes the legalization of one drug on the grounds that more and more drugs will inevitably be legalized as a consequence. It cannot be assumed that these other legalizations will take place simply because of this one, so the person is using the slippery slope fallacy, and choice A is correct. The other choices are incorrect because they refer to fallacies that are not being used here. A non sequitur (B) involves a conclusion that is not logically connected to a suggested cause (e.g., "He is rich, so he must be happy"). A red herring (C) introduces irrelevant information to distract attention from the actual issue. A straw man (D) misrepresents the opposing argument and then refutes the misrepresentation rather than the real argument.

109. C: Only choice C accurately describes a criterion for evaluating the credibility of a website as an information source. When viewing a website, it is necessary to watch for writer and publisher bias, as the writer and anyone with a stake in the success of the website may have their own agendas. Choice A is incorrect because the domain name of a website and the publisher of a website are both important to consider. Likewise, choice B is incorrect because whether the information on a website can be corroborated and how recently it has been updated are both important considerations for an online source's credibility. Choice D is incorrect because links to, citations of, and recommendations for other sources generally add credibility, particularly if the other sources are reliable or authoritative.

110. B: This is an example of the cause-and-effect structural pattern of informational text because it recounts the events leading up to World War I in a way that suggests how each event led to the next one by using words like "triggered," "in reaction to," "therefore," and "consequently." The descriptive pattern uses sensory imagery enabling readers to see, hear, feel, smell, and taste things; and/or tells readers the what, who, when, where, and why of the topic. The sequence and order pattern arranges events in chronological sequence, or gives instructions in the order to follow steps. Although this example also relates events in chronological sequence, it is a better example of cause and effect because each successive event is also attributed to the preceding one. The comparison-contrast pattern identifies the similarities and differences among things or ideas. (A fifth pattern is problem-solution.)

111. B: This is a compound–complex sentence because it includes a dependent clause ("After David met Marcia"), which cannot stand on its own as a sentence but depends on an independent clause, plus two independent clauses ("he knew she was the one" and "he soon proposed marriage to her") joined by a coordinating conjunction ("and"). A compound sentence has two independent clauses but no dependent clause. A complex sentence has at least one dependent clause and only one independent clause, not two. A simple sentence has only one independent clause and no dependent clauses.

112. C: Choice C is correct because *into small groups* is a prepositional phrase that modifies the phrasal verb *split up*. Choice A is incorrect because, even though *after* can be a preposition, in this case it is a subordinating conjunction because it is followed by a subject and a verb: *we arrive*. Choice B includes *up*, which can often be a preposition, but in this case is an adverb that forms the phrasal verb *split up*. Choice D is an infinitive functioning as an adverb to show the purpose of the main verb phrase *will split up*.

113. C: For internet sources, the name of the author can usually be found, but it may not be obvious at first. Therefore, choice C is correct; those wishing to cite the author may need to Internet search more thoroughly than usual to find the author's name. Nevertheless, they should not immediately assume the author is not named, so choice A is incorrect. Many internet sources are published by government agencies or private corporations and do not provide individual author names. In these cases, the writer should not list an author at all, so choice B is incorrect. Online sources omit authors' names much more commonly than do print sources. In these cases, citing the title in lieu of the author's name is not just allowed but advised by the MLA, so choice D is incorrect.

114. C: *Seldom* could describe either *hug* or *are shy*. The sentence should be rewritten as, "Children who seldom hug are shy," or "Children who hug are seldom shy."

115. B: Choice B is the only viable reason to use a particular regional dialect for narration in a novel, among these choices. The novel mentioned is narrated by the titular protagonist, who speaks in the dialect and lives in the place and time where this dialect was common. This reminds readers of the setting's significance to the novel and main character. It is unlikely that the author of a book published in 2000 would be most comfortable speaking a 1920s dialect, but even if they were, this would not be justification to have a character use the dialect, so choice A is not correct. While attracting readers' attention (C) and contrasting the narrator with other characters (D) are possible effects of the narrator speaking in this dialect, these are not strong reasons by themselves to choose a specific dialect for a narrator.

116. C: According to the Association of College and Research Libraries, information literacy is the set of skills that an individual must have for the finding, retrieval, analysis, and use of information. While it is required for reading and understanding information, it is required for more than this, so choice A is incorrect. It does not necessarily or exclusively involve retaining a lot of information or communicating information effectively, so choices B and D are incorrect. Rather, information literacy involves knowing how to find information, how to evaluate information critically, and how to apply information judiciously to meet specific purposes.

117. B: In the two-column notes active reading strategy, main ideas are noted in one of two columns while details are noted in the other column. The phrase "our fathers brought forth… a new nation" (B) would be considered the main idea and go in the main idea column. "Four score and seven years ago" (A), "conceived in Liberty" (C), and "dedicated to the proposition that all men are created equal" (D) are all details related to the central idea of a newly created nation.

118. A: *–tion* is a suffix because it comes at the end of a word. It turns a verb into a noun: *attend* becomes *attention, convert* becomes *conversion, present-presentation, converse-conversation, ambulate-ambulation,* and more. Prefixes, suffixes, and infixes are all affixes. However, *-tion* does not turn nouns into pronouns. Pronouns are *I, me, we, us, you, he, she, they, them, it* (personal pronouns); *this, that, these, those, such* (demonstrative pronouns); *who, whom, which, that* (relative pronouns); *somebody, anybody, everybody, each, every, all, some, none, one* (indefinite pronouns); *myself, ourselves, yourself, himself, herself, themselves* (intensive or reflexive pronouns); and many more. The *–tion* suffix does not come at beginnings of words and hence is not a prefix, and does not make nouns into verbs—such as *fright* into *frighten*—but vice versa. Infixes come in the middles of words, like *s* in *mothers-in-law* or *passers-by*; or in expressions like "abso-blooming-lutely" in *My Fair Lady. –tion* is not an infix and does not make a noun into an adjective, such as *danger* into *dangerous.*

119. A: Toni Morrison's novels focus on black women and their search for a place within American culture and society. She often uses fantasy to explore the themes of racism, gender bias, and class conflict. She is both a Nobel Prize and Pulitzer Prize winner. Her novels include *The Bluest Eye*, *Sula*, *Song of Solomon*, and *Beloved.*

120. A: The plot of a story is a set of events, and each event is impacted by a conflict that a character in the story is experiencing. Thus, conflict drives the plot of the story forward, and there cannot be a plot without some kind of conflict. Choice B is incorrect because, in most stories, the protagonist's goal is to resolve the main conflict. In fact, for many protagonists, their personal goals or troubles contribute to or form the main conflict. Choice C is incorrect because the impact that each type of conflict has on the plot depends on the story. Choice D is incorrect because the main conflict is generally resolved in the climax of a plot, not before it.

121. A: Departing from Aristotle's ancient Greek definitions, later aestheticians have defined the poetic genres of epic (sometimes referred to as narrative), lyric, and dramatic, so choice A is correct, and the other choices are incorrect. Contrary to Aristotle's definition of lyric poetry (which included being sung, being accompanied by a lyre, and having a specific meter), lyric poetry has a contemporary definition as poetry that expresses feelings. Epic and dramatic poetry have largely retained their definitions. Meanwhile, comic poetry and tragic poetry have come to be considered subgenres of dramatic poetry.

122. C: The clauses in the sentence are as follows: *Because he was late* is a dependent clause because it is introduced by the subordinating conjunction *because* and therefore cannot stand alone; *he missed the field trip* is an independent clause because it can stand alone as a sentence; *and this caused him to fail the class* is also an independent clause. Since there are two independent clauses and one dependent clause, choice C is correct, and the other choices are incorrect.

123. A: "Light" is the subject of the sentence. "From yonder window" is a prepositional phrase beginning with the preposition "from," then the adjective "yonder," modifying the object "window," an indirect object modifying the verb "breaks." Subject-verb-object is the typical syntax of most English sentences; Shakespeare changes this by placing the verb at the end of the sentence instead of after the subject and before the object as is most common.

124. D: The evaluator of a summary of a literary passage should consider whether the student's summary achieves an equal balance of concision and completeness, so (A) is incorrect. The student should also summarize the passage objectively and neutrally, excluding their own reactions or opinions, so (B) is incorrect. The summary should cover the passage's points in a similar proportion as the original text, so (C) is incorrect. Finally, the student should tag attributions of ideas to their original authors by name, cite the passage's original source so summary readers can find it, and avoid overusing quotations. This means (D) is the correct answer.

125. D: To evaluate source credibility, researchers consider not only an author's reputation in the field, but equally whether s/he cites sources. These two commonly (but not always) go hand-in-hand: generally, authors respected in their fields are responsible and cite sources. (In popular fields, some individuals gain favorable reputations without responsible scholarship. This is less common in rigorous academic fields.) In some rapidly changing fields, for instance information technologies, sources must be current; in others, such as 19th-century American history (barring new historical discoveries), information published decades ago may still be accurate. Researchers must consider author point of view and purpose, which affect neutrality. Sources from certain points of view can be credible, but may restrict subject treatment to one side of a debate. Audience values influence what they consider credible: younger readers accept Internet sources more, academics value refereed journals, and local community residents may value mainstream sources like *Newsweek* magazine.

126. A: Rubrics are useful not only for assessing student work but also for identifying learning objectives and guiding student work. Students can often improve the quality of their work by using the rubric to guide their writing, so (A) is the correct answer, and (C) is incorrect. Teachers should explain the rubric to students before they begin work to ensure students understand the assignment and how to read the rubric, making (B) incorrect. Rubrics should be designed based on learning objectives from lesson plans, rather than the other way around. This helps ensure that the assignment is relevant to what is being taught in class and adequately requires students to apply their knowledge. As a result, (D) is incorrect.

127. A: When a researcher has conducted an original experiment and reports the results, findings, and associated conclusions in a research report, that report is considered a primary source. Academic textbooks, journal articles, articles in other periodicals, and authoritative databases may all be primary sources. When an academic textbook cites research by others, that citation is considered a secondary source as it refers to information originally presented by others. When a news article quotes a researcher's writing, that is also a secondary source, as is a description given on a website of another person's research.

128. A: Teachers should generally use a variety of formal and informal assessment instruments to get a complete picture of student achievement. This is especially applicable for grouping students, which teachers should never do for the long term based on the results of only one assessment instrument. To conduct formative assessments of learning in progress, teachers should use both formal and informal test instruments; and use several different kinds, rather than choosing only one formal instrument to use exclusively. Formative assessment results are valuable not only for evaluating student progress, but moreover for use in the classroom as teaching tools.

129. B: Students should write appropriately to the specific occasion, purpose, and audience to ensure their particular readers will understand what they want to communicate. Therefore, writers in middle school grades should not use more advanced handwriting to set an example for younger readers (A); use longer, more complex sentences to give younger readers a challenge (C); or simply use their own typical levels to make their writing its most natural (D). They should instead use printing, simpler vocabulary and sentence structure, and shorter sentences on the level of readers in the early elementary grades. The primary goal is for the younger readers to understand the writing, so it should be at their reading levels.

130. C: Writers use a cause-and-effect structure to show how one event or idea is caused by or leads to another. Words such as *because* and *consequently* are useful in expressing a cause-and-effect relationship. Comparison and contrast is used to show how things are similar or different. In a problem and solution structure, the writer identifies a problem and then poses solutions. Writers may also arrange events in temporal sequence; that is, in the order in which they happen.

Practice Test #2

1. Which can we determine about the word *progress* from context clues in each sentence? Choose ALL correct answers.

"She has made remarkable progress as a student."
"After a good beginning, her work did not progress."

a. It is a noun in the first sentence.
b. It is an adjective in the second sentence.
c. It is a verb in the second sentence.
d. The second syllable is stressed in the first sentence.
e. The first syllable is stressed in the second sentence.

2. Which two kinds of writing commonly share the characteristic of using subjective, expressive language—among other techniques—to accomplish their purposes with reading audiences?

a. Speculative and persuasive
b. Descriptive and speculative
c. Persuasive and descriptive
d. Narrative and explanatory

3. Among the elements of a written argument, which one do statistics and examples most represent?

a. Claims
b. Reasons
c. Evidence
d. Counterclaims

4. Of the following components of a reference citation, which one is needed only for citing electronic sources rather than for both printed and electronic sources?

a. Author name
b. Publication date
c. Book/article title
d. The date of access

5. Which of the following sentences uses the word "smart" with a negative connotation, rather than a positive connotation or simply the word's denotation?

a. Eliot's teacher said he was not quite gifted, but too smart for a general class.
b. Eliot was smart to have studied the day before the test; he got a good grade.
c. Eliot was identified by his teacher as one of the smart students in her classes.
d. Eliot got into trouble when he gave a smart answer to his teacher's question.

6. Among effective research practices, which of the following is most accurate?

a. If one finds unlimited material, one should broaden one's research question.
b. If one finds too little related material, one's research question is too narrow.
c. If one knows the research question first, one can get lost among all the data.
d. If one finds no existing literature on a new topic, no type of searching helps.

7. Which mode of writing is most suitable for the purpose of encouraging the reading audience to explore ideas and consider various potential associated responses?

a. Narrative
b. Expository
c. Persuasive
d. Speculative

Refer to the following for questions 8–11:

The Thought-Fox

I imagine this midnight moment's forest:
Something else is alive
Beside the clock's loneliness
And this blank page where my fingers move.
Through the window I see no star:
Something more near
Though deeper within darkness
Is entering the loneliness:
Cold, delicately as the dark snow
A fox's nose touches twig, leaf;
Two eyes serve a movement, that now
And again now, and now, and now
Sets neat prints into the snow
Between trees, and warily a lame
Shadow lags by stump and in hollow
Of a body that is bold to come
Across clearings, an eye,
A widening deepening greenness,
Brilliantly, concentratedly,
Coming about its own business
Till, with a sudden sharp hot stink of fox,
It enters the dark hole of the head.
The window is starless still; the clock ticks,
The page is printed.

From *Ted Hughes: Selected Poems 1957-1967. Copyright © 1972 by Ted Hughes, Harper & Row Publishers, Inc.*

8. Which of the following literary devices is primarily used by the poet in this work?

a. Foreshadowing
b. Repetition
c. Metaphor
d. Irony

9. Which of these does the poem describe?

a. The process of observing a fox
b. The process of being inspired to write
c. The process of passing the time by thinking
d. The process of creating art from seeing nature

10. Which of the following best summarizes the creative writing process as described by the poem?

a. The writer carefully guides a thought.
b. The writer looks to nature for a thought.
c. The poet imagines a fox to help him to write.
d. The writer is a passive recipient of a thought.

11. In which of the following forms is this poem written?

a. Free verse
b. Blank verse
c. Rhymed verse
d. Metered verse

12. Based on assessment data, a teacher identifies a small group of students who would benefit from targeted instruction on using textual evidence to support their answers. Which strategy would be most helpful for the teacher to model to assist students with this type of test question?

a. Underlining passages in the text where answers are located
b. Reading the passage once to identify the main idea, and then rereading to look for details
c. Reading each answer choice carefully before selecting an answer, crossing out answers as they are eliminated
d. Completing a story map while reading the story

13. Which statement is most accurate about reader identification of author purpose in informational writing?

a. Considering why an author wrote a text affords greater insights to it.
b. Considering why an author wrote a text weakens critical reading skills.
c. Considering why an author wrote a text frees the reader from expectations.
d. Considering why an author wrote a text causes a weaker connection with the text.

14. Which of the following sentences uses metaphor?

a. In 1932, the shroud of the Great Depression was at its heaviest.
b. Hardships of the Great Depression continued to worsen in 1932.
c. The Great Depression's effects hung like a cloud over the year 1932.
d. The year 1932 saw new extremes in poverty due to the Great Depression.

15. Identify the grammatical error in the following sentence:

Growing up in the 60s and 70s, our neighborhood was safe enough to leave our doors unlocked.

a. Dangling participle
b. Split infinitive
c. Adjective/adverb confusion
d. Misplaced modifier

16. Early in the school year, all members of a group of kindergarten students are able to chant the alphabet. The teacher is now teaching the students what the alphabet looks like in written form. The teacher points to a letter, and the students vocalize the corresponding sound. Alternatively, the teacher vocalizes a phoneme and a student points to it on the alphabet chart. The teacher is using ____________ in her instruction.

a. letter–sound correspondence
b. rote memorization
c. predictive analysis
d. segmentation

17. Mark Twain famously included several distinctive versions of Southern US English in *Adventures of Huckleberry Finn* (1884). Which of the following are these versions of English examples of?

a. Jargon
b. Slang
c. Dialect
d. Accent

18. Which of the following can the writer determine without considering the audience?

a. Purpose
b. Structure
c. Word choice
d. Amount of research

19. Of the following, which sentence is correctly punctuated?

a. "I told you that it would be ready next week; it will be ready next week."
b. "I told you, that it would be ready next week it will be ready next week."
c. "I told you that it would be ready next week, it will be ready next week."
d. "I told you that it would be ready next week it will be ready next week."

20. *Since, therefore,* and *accordingly* are examples of which type of signal words?

a. Common, or basic, signal words
b. Compare/contrast words
c. Cause–effect words
d. Temporal sequencing words

21. Which of the following would be most useful in assessing and documenting students' language progress throughout a school year?

a. An audio/video recording of each student reading the same text at the beginning of the year and again at the end of the year
b. A portfolio including pre-tests, post-tests, vocabulary work, journal entries, writing assignments, group projects, and other relevant work from throughout the year
c. Score composites and details from state- and national-referenced exams or other standardized tests.
d. A detailed narrative composed by the student's teacher, detailing strengths, weaknesses, and descriptions of the student's work.

22. "She likes hiking, swimming, rowing, and to climb mountains." Which type of error does this sentence demonstrate?

a. A run-on sentence
b. A dangling participle
c. A sentence fragment
d. A lack of parallelism

23. Which of the following methods of connecting and distinguishing ideas considers both similarities and differences?

a. Correlating
b. Analogizing
c. Contrasting
d. Categorizing

24. Which of the following questions should be answered by the writer's thesis statement?

a. What is the subject of the essay?
b. What is the purpose of the essay?
c. How is the essay structured?
d. What does the essay attempt to prove?

25. Which of the following actions is NOT one that students must take in order to understand, critically judge, draw conclusions about, and individually interpret informational text that they read?

a. Locate evidence in texts
b. Connect texts with other texts
c. Make inferences about texts
d. Relate texts to prior knowledge

26. Which of the following is NOT a characteristic of a strong conclusion?

a. The conclusion highlights that the main points made were meaningful and important.
b. The conclusion includes a restating of the thesis or main argument of the piece.
c. The conclusion brings the work to the expected word count.
d. The conclusion reinforces the main points and reminds the reader how they are related.

27. Which of the following reflects MLA guidelines for citing internet sources with regard to page numbers in in-text citations in research papers?

a. A source from the internet should not be used if it does not include page numbers in any form.
b. If a printout from a website has page numbers, citations should include these numbers.
c. In-text citations of online sources in research papers should never include page numbers.
d. If the source is a PDF file, the page numbers from the file should be in citations.

28. In the word transcontinental, what does the prefix trans most nearly mean?

a. Across
b. Change
c. Carrying
d. Different

29. Which of the following sentences contains a simile?

a. Joe could feel the butterflies in his stomach as he waited backstage.
b. Our company has many opportunities for those climbing the career ladder.
c. These chairs have an innovative design that makes you feel as light as a feather.
d. The year started off strong for us, as we hit our sales targets for the first quarter.

30. "Courage, determination, and perseverance is required for success in this effort." What is grammatically incorrect in this sentence?

a. There is nothing wrong
b. Subject-verb agreement
c. Agreement of verb tense
d. Lack of parallel structure

31. Suppose an informational text on the writer's craft presents a list of common errors in essay writing along with the consequences of these errors and steps writers can take in order to avoid committing these errors themselves. Which of these text structures would this informational text most likely follow?

a. Process narrative
b. Cause and effect
c. Problem-solution
d. Description

32. What is a primary purpose for giving an Informal Reading Inventory to a student?

a. To track the texts and genres a student has read over the course of the school year
b. To help students identify books of personal interest
c. To determine which reading behaviors students have developed prior to entering formal schooling
d. To match students with appropriate instructional texts

33. When students are taught to use effective reading comprehension strategies, one of the benefits is that they learn to think about how they think when they read, a process or skill known as which of the following?

a. Schemata
b. Scaffolding
c. Metacognition
d. Metamorphosis

34. Teachers must establish clear ground rules before initiating class or group discussions to ensure that students practice active listening and productive participation. Which of the following rules is more applicable to young children and students with behavior disorders than to all students equally?

a. No cross-talk
b. No interrupting
c. No monopolizing discussions
d. No hitting, kicking, biting, etc.

35. Which of the following statements adheres to Information Literacy Standards?

a. Students accessing information must critically evaluate it and its sources before using it.
b. Students accessing information should acquire as much information as possible about their topic.
c. Students accessing information efficiently sacrifice incidental learning.
d. Students accessing information must avoid using it for purposes it was not meant to serve.

36. Which of the following sentences is an appeal to emotion?

a. Using a cell phone while driving is dangerous, as you have to steer with one hand.
b. It is really stupid to use a cell phone when you drive because it is so dangerous.
c. Statistics conclusively show that using a cell phone while driving is dangerous.
d. Many places have driving laws that ban the use of a cell phone while driving.

37. In digital media, which of these advantages do cross-media transformations provide?

a. Students can underline all summary sentences in detailed texts.
b. Teachers can italicize all words in a text with Greek or Latin roots.
c. Students can boldface new or unfamiliar vocabulary words in a text.
d. Teachers and students can convert speech to text and text to speech.

Refer to the following for question 38:

For a poetry unit, a class is reading a 14-line poem in iambic pentameter. There are three stanzas of four lines each, and a two-line couplet at the end. Words at the end of each line rhyme with another word in the same stanza. After the first week of this unit, the teacher wants to determine if the instructional methods she is using are successful. If students are meeting the objectives introduced so far, she will continue with the strategies she is currently using. If students are struggling to meet the objectives, she will reteach them using a different approach. For the assessment, she plans to ask students to identify the literary devices she has introduced in sample poems.

38. Which type of assessment is the teacher planning to use?

a. Formative assessment
b. Summative assessment
c. Norm-referenced test
d. Screening assessment

39. When creating an outline, it is important to use:

a. Prepositions
b. Progressivism
c. Abbreviation
d. Subordination

40. Regarding literal versus figurative language in informational texts, the words "politician" and "statesman" have which of the following?

a. Both the same denotation and connotation
b. Both different denotations and connotations
c. The same denotation but different connotations
d. The same connotation but different denotations

41. Which of the following is true of the introduction to a written piece?

a. It is best to write it first.
b. It is best to write it last.
c. It should reinforce the points made in the piece.
d. It is the least important part of a piece of writing.

42. Which of the following is an accurate statement about text coding (Harvey and Daniels, 2009) as an active reading strategy?

a. Text coding refers to having students write computer code.
b. Text coding is a strategy that some also call text monitoring.
c. Text coding and text monitoring are two different strategies.
d. Text coding can be done by students with no teacher model.

43. Which choice is the most correct statement about mood and tone in literature?

a. Mood and tone are synonyms referring to the emotional atmosphere of the work.
b. Mood is the emotion evoked in the reader by the work; tone is the author's emotion.
c. Mood is the emotion expressed by a work's author; tone is the emotion evoked in the reader by the work.
d. Mood is established by authors using different literary techniques than those used in creating tone.

44. "He could not finish the test in time even though he tried his hardest." This sentence is of which type?

a. Compound–complex
b. Compound
c. Complex
d. Simple

45. Which of the following is a primary function of argumentative writing?

a. To explain a process to readers
b. To articulate a concept for readers
c. To present new information to readers
d. To prove a point that will convince readers

46. If an author of informational text makes a reference to someone famous, e.g., the name of a literary or historical figure, to create resonance with readers and/or make something or someone in the text symbolic, what rhetorical device is this?

a. Allusion
b. Paradox
c. Analogy
d. Parody

47. A student is taking a reading test. The teacher has blocked out a number of words. Each blank is assigned a set of three possible words. The student must select the correct word from each set so that the text makes sense. The student is taking:

a. A cloze test
b. A maze test
c. A multiple-choice quiz
d. A vocabulary test

48. Of the following words, which is NOT an example of onomatopoeia?

a. *Hum*
b. *Click*
c. *Buzz*
d. *Moan*

49. Which of the following uses figurative meaning rather than literal meaning?

a. The willow tree is weeping into the stream.
b. The willow tree's leaves are narrow and pointed.
c. The willow tree has flexible branches that trail.
d. The willow tree's long branches sway in the wind.

50. Which of the following is true of *The Adventures of Huckleberry Finn* by Mark Twain, *The Diary of a Young Girl* by Anne Frank, and "The Fall of the House of Usher" by Edgar Allan Poe?

a. They are all examples of narrative writing.
b. They are all fictional retellings of events that occurred in real life.
c. They are all social commentaries that were once considered radical.
d. They are all written in the third-person omniscient narrative viewpoint.

51. Which of the following mediums is NOT often written in the second-person?

a. Novels
b. Song lyrics
c. Advertisements
d. Instruction manuals

52. Of the following statements, which one accurately reflects a principle related to integrating source material into research writing?

a. Parenthetically naming studies that agree/disagree with one's position interrupts an argument.
b. If students cannot write an equal/larger number of words about a quotation, it is likely padding.
c. When quoting sources, students should follow quotations with summaries of what these mean.
d. Summarizing others' content is as engaging and original as analyses, syntheses, and evaluations.

53. When an author uses rhetoric to support his or her point of view or purpose in an informational text, by which of these means can they best provide supporting evidence?

a. Relating personal anecdotes
b. Making analogies to clarify ideas
c. Describing relevant case studies
d. Laying out premises and conclusions

54. The statements below exhibit which of the following grammatical errors?

> Many literary scholars also point to the traditions of the Welsh story collection known as the *Mabinogion* for the origins. And even the name of the legendary King Arthur.

a. Incorrectly placed comma
b. Incorrect use of capitalization
c. Incomplete sentence
d. There is no error

55. Of the following criteria for critically evaluating how effective an informational text author's methods of appealing to the reading audience are, which is related to whether readers believed the author, and why they did or did not?

a. Clarity
b. Accuracy
c. Cohesion
d. Credibility

56. Where does a suffix appear in a word?

a. at the beginning
b. at the end
c. in the middle
d. any place

57. Which of these should readers do to evaluate the arguments of informational texts?

a. Identify only assumptions that the author has included in the argument.
b. Word any assumptions identified only from the perspective of a reader.
c. Check if the premises and conclusion in a deductive argument are true.
d. Test for the validity of an argument made based on inductive reasoning.

58. Middle school students at Ms. Kelso's school are expected to complete a large independent study project to be presented at the end of the second term. The project is the culmination of reading research, writing a paper, and the final element of publishing, or presentation. The students can choose how they present their work and are instructed to use visual aids. Which of the following would be a helpful guideline for Ms. Kelso to offer her students?

a. Whenever possible, use pictures, video, music, charts and graphs to supplement your presentation for the purpose of keeping your audience's interest.
b. Think about any parts of your paper that might be hard to explain. Choose a visual aid to help you show your audience the concept, and then use your words to explain it.
c. Select the most interesting photographs from your research, create color photocopies, and pass them throughout the class during your presentation.
d. Use your main ideas and supporting evidence to create a Power-point slideshow, making note-taking and organization simple and clear.

59. Which of the following is true of literary character development?

a. Whether a character is dynamic or static is irrelevant to their development.
b. The main character's development throughout a story is usually the result of a conflict.
c. Round characters do not experience any development in a story.
d. Foils are used to make a main character's traits less obvious.

60. Which of the following statements is true about TV and radio as types of media for communicating ideas?

a. TV is a high-status mass medium, but radio is not.
b. TV does not have as broad of a reach as radio does.
c. TV and radio can both serve to raise awareness.
d. TV targets more specific audiences than radio.

61. Which of the following statements is true regarding paragraphs that have been inadequately developed?

a. They provide needed background.
b. They are unconvincing and ineffective.
c. They always demonstrate poor writing.
d. They never include required information.

62. Which of the following sentences uses implicit rather than explicit meaning?

a. The student, her face pale, said, "We didn't finish the test."
b. The students panicked just because they were not able to finish the test.
c. The students were unable to finish the test in the time allotted.
d. The students so dreaded failing the test that their faces had paled.

63. In three pieces of informational writing, Sample 1's author provides evidence tangential to his argument. Sample 2's author cites anecdotal evidence which is inaccurate. Sample 3's author cites accurate, directly related evidence, but it is an isolated example uncorroborated by any other sources. Which choice correctly matches each sample to the evidence criterion it fails to meet?

a. Sample 1's evidence is not sufficient, Sample 2's is not relevant, and Sample 3's is not factual.
b. Sample 1's evidence is not factual, Sample 2's is not sufficient, and Sample 3's is not relevant.
c. Sample 1's evidence is not relevant, Sample 2's is not factual, and Sample 3's is not sufficient.
d. Samples 1 and 3's evidence is insufficient, and Sample 2's is factual but irrelevant

64. In the novel *The Great Gatsby* by F. Scott Fitzgerald, Jay Gatsby has climbed the social ladder from humble beginnings into great wealth and status, yet he is not content. From outside his house, a distant green light across the bay is visible. Gatsby knows it is the light at the end of the dock owned by Daisy, his love interest, who is already married. Throughout the story, he stares reflectively at the light, sometimes for prolonged periods, and even reaches out for it. Which of the following statements best describes the author's use of the green light?

a. It foreshadows a love affair.
b. It symbolizes unattainable desires.
c. It provides a metaphor for chasing wealth.
d. It highlights the distance between Gatsby and Daisy.

65. What is an accurate reflection of criteria for clear, concise speech presentations?

a. A speaker should not take three or more minutes more to get to the point.
b. A speaker should not pause before answering audience questions.
c. A speaker should include as many anecdotes and details as possible.
d. A speaker should include both necessary and interesting information.

66. Which of the following sentences is most likely a topic sentence of a supporting paragraph?

a. Another danger it presents is the accumulation of tiny plastic particles in groundwater.
b. The three largest threats are overuse of plastic, dumping of industrial waste, and excessive carbon emission.
c. Finally, the single largest environmental problem today is excessive carbon emission, which has several consequences.
d. Everyone can begin to make a difference today not only by doing their part but by taking the time to understand these threats themselves.

67. Which of the following sentences is punctuated correctly?

a. Not all permission slips were returned, moreover the bus was unavailable.
b. Not all permission slips were returned; moreover, the bus was unavailable.
c. Not all permission slips were returned, moreover; the bus was unavailable.
d. Not all permission slips were returned, moreover, the bus was unavailable.

68. Which of the following sentences is grammatically correct?

a. You're nametag is in it's place on the table.
b. Your nametag is in it's place on the table.
c. You're nametag is in its place on the table.
d. Your nametag is in its place on the table.

69. What is one benefit of using a rubric over other types of assessment techniques?

a. Rubrics break down overall scores by criteria, allowing students to see their strengths and weaknesses.
b. Rubrics allow students to track their progress over time.
c. Rubrics help students see how they did in comparison with their peers.
d. Rubrics help identify the types of reading miscues students are making so teachers can provide targeted instruction.

70. In an analogy comparing an essay to a table, how would parts of the table correspond to parts of the essay?

a. Each leg is a main idea while the top is all of the supporting evidence.
b. The top is the main idea, and each leg is a group of supporting details.
c. Each leg is one paragraph, and the top of the table is the central idea.
d. The top is the introductory paragraph, and the legs are all the other paragraphs.

71. Which of the following statements accurately reflects research findings on effective instruction for developing student vocabulary?

a. To understand specific texts, lessons, or subjects, students need direct vocabulary instruction.
b. To retain newly learned vocabulary words, students need multiple, repeated exposures via drilling.
c. To increase productive language skills, students need to be taught low-frequency vocabulary words.
d. To accommodate faster learning, teachers should keep the structures of vocabulary exercises constant.

72. Which of the following is NOT a clause?

a. He died.
b. It's raining.
c. A very good time
d. Then we went out

73. Use the following sentence to answer the question.

I would like to go with you; however, I won't have time.

In this sentence, what part of speech is the word "however"?

a. Adverb
b. Pronoun
c. Preposition
d. Conjunction

74. A teacher helps students analyze informational text to see how authors connect and distinguish ideas by giving them sentence frames. For example, "_____ are _____, meaning they eat _____." Students fill these in, such as "Rabbits are herbivores, meaning they eat only plants" or "Frogs are carnivores, meaning they eat only meat." These are examples of which of the following?

a. Making analogies among animals
b. Grouping animals into categories
c. Comparing animals by similarities
d. Contrasting animals' differences

75. The short story "Twenty-Six Men and a Girl" by Maxim Gorky is about twenty-six bakers whose only joy during the workday is a girl who visits for baked goods. The story is told by one of the bakers, from his own perspective. What point of view is this?

a. First person
b. Second person
c. Limited third person
d. Omniscient third person

76. Which of the following is NOT one of the purposes of the conclusion in an essay?

a. To summarize the main points in the body of the essay
b. To clarify the context or application of the essay content
c. To reiterate the thesis that was stated in the introduction
d. To include important material that would not fit elsewhere

77. When writing a research paper on an English literature topic, which of the following styles should generally be used?

a. MLA style
b. APA style
c. Chicago style
d. AMA style

78. A teacher wants his students to become familiar with a wide range of genres and text structures. Which of the following options would best help him achieve this goal?

a. Displaying posters describing different genres and text structures in the classroom
b. Rewarding students who choose to read a variety of different types of books during independent reading time
c. Selecting books from different genres and with different text structures for read-alouds and shared reading activities
d. Sending home a list of varied books and encouraging students to check them out from their local libraries

Refer to the following for question 79:

There Will Come Soft Rains

By Sara Teasdale

There will come soft rains and the smell of the ground,
And swallows circling with their shimmering sound;

And frogs in the pools singing at night,
And wild plum trees in tremulous white;

Robins will wear their feathery fire
Whistling their whims on a low fence-wire;

And not one will know of the war, not one
Will care at last when it is done.

Not one would mind, neither bird nor tree
If mankind perished utterly;

And Spring herself, when she woke at dawn,
Would scarcely know that we were gone.

79. Which line is the best example of personification used in the poem?

a. "And frogs in the pools singing at night"
b. "Robins will wear their feathery fire"
c. "And not one will know of the war, not one"
d. "And Spring herself, when she woke at dawn"

80. Of the following types of sources, which would most likely need to have an access date included in its citation?

a. A book
b. A legal document
c. A trade magazine article
d. A journal article published online

81. In character development analysis, which of the following is NOT likely to be helpful?

a. Paying attention to observations the narrator makes about a character
b. Observing apparent contradictions in a character's thoughts and behavior
c. Determining how a character could be used differently by the author
d. Noting how the narrator and the other characters speak differently about a character

82. Edna St. Vincent Millay has written, "Search the fading letters finding / Steadfast in the broken binding / All that once was I!" If the last line were rearranged into more common everyday syntax, how would it read?

a. All that I was once
b. Once I was all that
c. That I once all was
d. That all I was once

83. In poetry, poems in which form are the shortest?

a. Ode
b. Epic
c. Elegy
d. Epigram

84. Which of the following phrases is an example of using diction to convey a subjective connotation?

a. a heavy desk
b. a greasy smile
c. a blue sky
d. a formal speech

85. When students are writing the conclusions of their essays, which of the following should they do?

a. Paraphrase their main thesis statement
b. Repeat their main thesis statement verbatim
c. Apologize for their opinions and/or their writing
d. Always summarize their essay in every conclusion

86. In a rough draft of an essay, a student has written, "My best friend Gina is a wonderful athlete, a wonderful student, a wonderful person, and a wonderful friend." Which online reference should she consult to improve this description?

a. A grammar guide
b. An encyclopedia
c. A dictionary
d. A thesaurus

87. Which of the following authors was a 19th-century British novelist and short-story writer?

a. O. Henry
b. Charles Dickens
c. Herman Melville
d. Nathaniel Hawthorne

88. Which of the following best represents a main theme in William Shakespeare's *Romeo and Juliet*?

a. Fate does not control those who resist it.
b. Teenage love will always result in tragedy.
c. Defying society may have fatal consequences.
d. We cannot see the flaws in the people who we love.

89. An author whose YA novel has been optioned for a movie visits a class and talks about the steps involved in having a book produced as a movie. Which would be the final step?

a. The author begins with an idea or concept and sends a proposal to a movie producer.
b. A scriptwriter writes a script based on the novel.
c. The movie producer (and sometimes the writer) fleshes out a narrative describing how the concept will be adapted to the screen. This is called a treatment.
d. The movie producer pitches the treatment to a film company.

90. "He went to the ______ in order to ______ what happened." By applying knowledge of syntax, which of these could the reader determine?

a. The parts of speech of the missing words
b. The specific words for filling in the blanks
c. The reader can determine neither of these.
d. The reader could determine both of these.

91. The following sentence is which of the following sentence types?

The questions in this test can give you an idea of what kinds of questions you might find on the actual test; however, they are not duplicates of the actual test questions, which cover the same subject material but may differ in form and content.

a. Simple
b. Complex
c. Compound
d. Compound-complex

92. According to research into vocabulary instruction methods, which of the following aspects is NOT identified as requiring further investigation?

a. Receptive vocabulary vs. productive vocabulary
b. Written and print vocabulary vs. spoken vocabulary
c. Vocabulary definitions vs. vocabulary contexts
d. Depth of vocabulary vs. breadth of vocabulary

Refer to the following for questions 93–95:

> Mamzelle Aurélie possessed a good strong figure, ruddy cheeks, hair that was changing from brown to gray, and a determined eye. She wore a man's hat about the farm, and an old blue army overcoat when it was cold, and sometimes top-boots.
>
> Mamzelle Aurélie had never thought of marrying. She had never been in love. At the age of twenty she had received a proposal, which she had promptly declined, and at the age of fifty she had not yet lived to regret it.
>
> She was quite alone in the world, except for her dog Ponto, and the negroes who lived in her cabins and worked her crops, and the fowls, a few cows, a couple of mules, her gun (with which she shot chicken-hawks), and her religion.
>
> Excerpted from "Regret" by Kate Chopin, 1894

93. What can the reader infer about the main character from reading the passage above?

a. She is a single woman with many personal virtues but is also naïve.
b. She is a self-reliant, independent person who values being in control.
c. She is a shy and lonely farmer who has difficulty attracting suitors.
d. She is a cruel sociopath who is unable to acknowledge emotion.

94. Which of these quotes from the passage, along with the title of the piece, foreshadows later changes?

a. "She wore a man's hat about the farm, and an old blue army overcoat when it was cold"
b. "she had not yet lived to regret it"
c. "except for her dog Ponto"
d. "her gun (with which she shot chicken-hawks)"

95. Based on the passage, which of the following ideas is most likely central to this story?

a. Women who do not get married will always end up being lonely.
b. Gun ownership is an essential element of being independent.
c. Self-sufficiency is useful but, in excess, can lead to loneliness.
d. Experiencing what you were missing can relieve regret.

96. Which of the following suffixes is commonly used to form either an adjective or a noun from another part of speech?

a. *-ation*
b. *-ness*
c. *-ity*
d. *-al*

97. Which statement most accurately represents how evidence-based instructional approaches should be evaluated for effectiveness?

a. During the evaluation, assessors define the teaching practices that were used.
b. Ongoing monitoring is unnecessary because the evaluation identifies practices.
c. Appropriate, established measures are used to evaluate student results.
d. Student progress can be assessed without comparing teaching methods.

98. Which of the following statements describes how speculative writing is different from expository and argumentative writing?

a. Speculative writing combines the goals of expository and argumentative writing.
b. Speculative writing is less factual than exposition and less imaginative than persuasion.
c. Speculative writing makes fewer clear points than expository and argumentative writing.
d. Speculative writing typically uses tighter organization than expository and argumentative writing.

99. Which of the following is the best definition of paragraph cohesion?

a. Each idea is supported with solid evidence.
b. The ideas fit together and flow from one to the next.
c. A topic sentence starts the paragraph, and a closing sentence ends it.
d. All the sentences in the paragraph include appropriate transition words.

100. Which version of this sentence is most correctly punctuated and worded?

a. "Discussing the plan, Maddie and David disagreed, they often had differences of opinion."
b. "Discussing the plan, Maddie and David disagreed; they often had differences of opinion."
c. "Discussing the plan, Maddie and David disagreed. They often had differences of opinion."
d. "Discussing the plan, Maddie and David disagreed; and they often had differences of opinion."

101. Which of the following is an example of a complex sentence?

a. I do not have the time, although I would like to go with you.
b. I would like to go with you; however, I do not have the time.
c. I would like to be able to make the time to go out with you.
d. I'd go, and I'd go with you, if only I could just make the time.

102. A teacher designs lessons for the upcoming week. During the first part of the week, the teacher is going to divide the class into two sections. While one group is working independently on their projects, the other group will sit in a circle. The teacher has broken a story up into several sections, and each student will read a section aloud. The teacher will note for her records how many errors a student makes. She will also administer a brief verbal "quiz" to which the students will respond in writing. The combination of verbal reading results and comprehension quiz results will give her a better understanding of each child's abilities and/or needs. What kind of assessment did this teacher use?

a. Cloze-style
b. Informal reading inventory
c. Student response form
d. Articulation assessment

103. A teacher asked his students to prepare a presentation that could be shown in a foreign country. He advised them to

a. use idioms.
b. avoid anecdotes local to the foreign country.
c. avoid quotes from a foreign national of the country.
d. keep the presentation simple and succinct.

104. Which of the following is NOT a criterion for evaluating the strength of an analysis that is based on textual evidence?

a. The analysis explains the author's intended meaning or purpose.
b. The analysis uses strong, relevant, and accurate evidence for support.
c. The analysis includes specific evidence, such as paraphrasing or direct quotes.
d. The analysis shows special insight into a theme, character, or story event.

105. Identify the grammatical error in the following sentence:

They liked to stay at home, cook dinner, and watching TV.

a. Lack of parallelism
b. Split infinitive
c. Squinting modifier
d. Subject-verb disagreement

106. A student who is a non-native speaker of English hands in a composition that includes the following sentences:

Yesterday I go to the park. I have a good time swimming on the pool.

Which kinds of errors did the student make?

a. Subject/verb agreement and word order
b. Verb tense and preposition use
c. Misplaced modifier and sentence fragment
d. Pronoun error and dangling modifier

107. Which of the following reading strategies is LEAST likely to be effective in supporting active reading for students before they read?

a. Guessing what will happen
b. Drawing a story map of predictions
c. Summarizing current knowledge of the topic
d. Identifying questions that the text may answer

Refer to the following for question 108:

"Nancy also felt that the party was too crowded, but the hosts, who relied so much on her, would have been hurt if she had not attended."

108. In the sentence above, which parts are the independent clauses?

a. "Nancy also felt..."; "who relied so much on her"
b. "Nancy also felt..."; "the hosts would have been hurt..."
c. "who relied so much on her"; "if she had not attended"
d. "that the party was too crowded"; "who relied so much on her"

Refer to the following for question 109:

Come live with me and be my love,
And we will all the pleasures prove
That valleys, groves, hills, and fields,
Woods, or steepy mountain yields.

109. Consider that this poem uses pronunciation from Elizabethan English (late 1500s). What is the rhyme scheme of this stanza?

a. ABAB
b. ABBA
c. AABB
d. ABCD

110. Which of these is most accurate regarding persuasive techniques used in advertising?

a. Repetition and appeals to audience sentiment are both effective persuasive tools.
b. Qualifiers, better known as "weasel words," typically accompany understated claims.
c. Persuasion via humor is used more often in news and advocacy than in advertising.
d. Hyperbole, superlatives, and intensifiers are considered hallmarks of cheap advertising.

111. Among these forms of electronic media, which have the highest level of formality?

a. Online news articles
b. Online blogs
c. Emails
d. All are the same

112. What literary movement is a type of realistic fiction that developed in France, America and England in late the 19th century?

a. Romanticism
b. Realism
c. Naturalism
d. Classicism

113. The term *soliloquy* is used to refer to an element typically found in which literary genre/subgenre?

a. Drama
b. Poetry
c. Novels
d. Essays

114. Of the following, which is true about both *The Diary of a Young Girl* by Anne Frank (1947) and *Go Ask Alice* by Beatrice Sparks (1971), in addition to the fact that both are written in diary form?

a. They both are the diaries of 20th-century teenage girls.
b. They both are fictional novels created by the authors.
c. They both communicate negative perspectives on life.
d. They both end with the survival of the main character.

115. Among these procedural devices that help students plan and revise writing, which is helpful as an aid for remembering key sets of information?

a. Outlines
b. Checklists
c. Mnemonic devices
d. Graphic organizers

116. Which of the following statements is most accurate regarding passive voice as it relates to paragraph cohesion?

a. The passive voice makes paragraphs less cohesive.
b. The passive voice can be useful for paragraph cohesion.
c. The passive voice is critical for making paragraphs cohesive.
d. The passive voice should only be used when necessary.

Refer to the following for questions 117–119:

Because I could not stop for Death —
He kindly stopped for me —
The Carriage held but just Ourselves —
And Immortality.

We slowly drove — He knew no haste
And I had put away
My labor and my leisure too,
For His Civility —

We passed the School, where Children strove
At Recess — in the Ring —
We passed the Fields of Gazing Grain —
We passed the Setting Sun —

Or rather — He passed Us —
The Dews drew quivering and chill —
For only Gossamer, my Gown —
My Tippet — only Tulle —

We paused before a House that seemed
A Swelling of the Ground —
The Roof was scarcely visible —
The Cornice — in the Ground —

Since then — 'tis Centuries — and yet
Feels shorter than the Day
I first surmised the Horses' Heads
Were toward Eternity —

117. Throughout the poem, which of the following literary devices is used to describe death?

a. Analogy
b. Hyperbole
c. Alliteration
d. Personification

118. Which of the following best describes the tone of this poem?

a. Serious, grave, and portentously dark
b. Detached and alienated, with a numb, despairing feeling
c. Lighthearted, humorous, and gently ironic
d. Frantic and agitated, with a frenzy of fear

119. What is implicitly described in the fifth stanza?

a. A home
b. A grave
c. A church
d. A school

120. Regarding these elements of print awareness in literacy development, which is true?

a. All students with normal development can differentiate printed words from spaces.
b. To identify initial and final letters in words, students must identify words vs. spaces.
c. The only students not automatically knowing left-right directionality are certain ELLs.
d. Being able to identify basic punctuation is not important to reading comprehension.

121. Which of these statements about figurative language in informational text is accurate?

a. Literal language is to denotation as figurative language is to connotation.
b. Due to the purpose of informational text, there is no place for figurative language in it.
c. Both literal and figurative language must be used for effective informational text.
d. Informational text only uses literal language and only word denotations.

122. In text coding and text monitoring, which of the following codes means that the student is "really confused" about something in an informational text?

a. ??
b. ?
c. L
d. RR

123. Which of the following purposes should be the writer's primary focus in the body of an essay?

a. To argue for the credibility of the thesis
b. To clarify the meanings of unfamiliar words
c. To provide a lesson, extended thought, or takeaway
d. To make generalizations based on specific facts

124. Use the following sentence to answer this question.

Although Ted had an impressive education, he had little work experience, which presented a challenge during his job search.

How many dependent and independent clauses does this sentence contain?

a. No dependent clauses and two independent clauses
b. One dependent clause and two independent clauses
c. One dependent clause and one independent clause
d. Two dependent clauses and one independent clause

125. Which of the following aspects of poetic form is characteristic of haiku?

a. A 5-7-5 syllable pattern
b. An ABA rhyme scheme
c. Perfectly regular meter
d. Lengthy epic narratives

126. When is it most appropriate for students to write in casual language at their own age level?

a. To share a certain experience with their readers
b. To get parental permission for a desired activity
c. To write something for their classmates to read
d. To write a story that younger children can read

127. Of the following writing practices, which will interfere with producing a good paragraph?

a. Confine the content of each paragraph to only one main idea
b. Develop the main idea in a paragraph by giving specific details
c. Include a great many supporting details: the more, the better
d. Use a specific structural pattern to develop each paragraph

128. Which of the following choices will be most important when designing a reading activity or lesson for students?

a. Selecting a text
b. Determining the number of students participating
c. Analyzing the point in the school year at which the lesson is given
d. Determining a purpose for instruction

129. Which of the following purposes of writing is NOT a common purpose of journal writing?

a. Documenting experiences with an illness
b. Chronicling recovery from an addiction
c. Describing travels or figurative journeys
d. Relating stories of fictional characters

130. Which of the following is most accurate about the relationship between the physics of thinking and speaking as these inform classroom instruction in listening actively?

a. Because thinking outpaces speech, students' minds wander, so listening is less effective than reading.
b. The disparity between speaking and thinking speeds is conducive to active listening via summarizing.
c. The process of listening is an inherently social interaction; the process of learning is not equally social.
d. The process of learning is essentially a reciprocal one, but the process of listening is not as reciprocal.

Answer Key and Explanations for Test #2

1. A, C: We can tell from the context that in the first sentence, *progress* is a noun because it is the object of the verb "has made" and is modified by the adjective "remarkable." The object of the verb cannot be another verb, and adjectives modify nouns, not verbs. The noun "progress" is pronounced with the first syllable stressed. From the context, we can tell that in the second sentence *progress* is a verb because it modifies the noun subject "work." Nouns do not modify other nouns, and the subject needs a verb. The verb *progress* is pronounced with the second syllable stressed.

2. C: Persuasive or argumentative writing uses a combination of logic, proof, supporting evidence, and subjective, expressive language to influence reader feelings and beliefs. Descriptive writing also appeals to reader emotions, as well as reader imaginations and senses, by vividly portraying sensory details to recreate experiences, events, and scenes so that readers feel they are also experiencing what is described. Speculative writing does not aim to convince readers as persuasive writing does. It does not aim to recreate experiences for readers as descriptive writing does. Rather, speculative writing invites readers to explore diverse ideas and their potential outcomes. As such, it uses looser structure and less definitive points than persuasive or expository writing. Narrative writing aims primarily to tell a story. This may include affecting reader feelings through subjective, expressive language. However, explanatory writing does not share this characteristic; it aims to inform readers and explain information to them.

3. C: Statistics cited and examples given most represent evidence that writers supply to support the claims they make in written arguments. Claims (A) are the writer's basic positions regarding the topic. Reasons (B) also support claims as evidence does; however, evidence involves statistics, specific examples, or other facts from different sources that demonstrate the claim's validity, whereas reasons are given by the writer (e.g., for a claim that overusing digital devices causes harm, a reason could be that texting while driving causes accidents). Counterclaims (D) are claims that refute/oppose/contradict given claims.

4. D: When citing electronic sources, researchers must include the date they accessed the source in their references. When citing both printed and electronic sources, researchers must include the name of the author (A), the date of publication (B), and the title of the book or article (C).

5. D: This use of "smart" has a negative connotation: "a smart answer" here means a disrespectful or impertinent one. This is evident from the sentence context ("Eliot got into trouble"). The word "smart" has a literal denotation meaning intelligent or competent. "Smart" also has a positive connotation meaning wise or judicious. The context "he got a good grade" informs this use: Eliot was smart to have studied, meaning he used good judgment when he prepared, evidenced by the positive outcome.

6. B: If a researcher finds too little material about a research question, s/he should broaden the question, which may be too narrow to yield enough literature. If there is an unmanageable, seemingly unlimited amount of literature, s/he likely needs to narrow, not broaden the research question because it is too general. Many people voluntarily doing research enjoy information and can get overwhelmed by all the data they find. Knowing the research question in advance can keep the wealth of information from impeding progress. On new topics, sometimes no research literature exists yet. This does not mean that no type of searching helps: doing systematic searches can help, for example, first through periodical abstracts to get an overview of literature related to the topic, then through references cited in specific sources like individual research papers, and/or references cited in general sources like books about specific related topics.

7. D: The purpose of narrative writing (A) is to entertain readers with a story. Even when authors want to offer insights or teach lessons while entertaining readers, they accomplish this through storytelling. The purpose of expository writing (B) is to inform or direct readers. The purpose of persuasive writing (C) is to convince readers to agree with the author's position or argument. The purpose of speculative writing (D) is to encourage readers to explore ideas and potential responses rather than entertain, tell stories, inform, explain, direct, or convince.

8. C: Author Ted Hughes uses extended metaphor by describing the concrete presence of a fox to represent the abstract concept of a writer's inspiration. From beyond the blank window, in the dark forest, the fox approaches like a thought comes to mind, leaving pawprints in the snow the way that a thought may lead to letters on a page. Because the entire poem is a metaphor, choice C is correct. Foreshadowing (A) is a literary device where the writer hints at something that will become more apparent later in a story. Though the poem includes the use of repetition (B), this is not the primary literary device used. Irony (D) is a literary device where the writer creates a noticeable difference between what is said in a story and what happens in it.

9. B: The poem describes how the speaker is inspired to write, using the fox to embody a thought that enters the speaker's mind, hence the title "The Thought-Fox". It does not describe an actual fox or the process of observing one, so choice A is incorrect. Though the poem notes the ticking clock, it does not describe the process of merely passing the time, so choice C is incorrect. The poem describes the creative process and uses a metaphor from nature to do this, but it does not describe the specific process of creating from the inspiration of nature, so choice D is incorrect.

10. D: The speaker's passivity and lack of control over the thought that inspires his or her writing can be interpreted from Ted Hughes's description of the thought as a fox that approaches unbidden, from outside, out of a blank nothingness. This passivity is emphasized by the description of the Thought-Fox as "Coming about its own business." Therefore, choice D is correct. The speaker as a passive recipient is further shown in the last stanza, where the fox "enters the dark hole of the head," and in the last line, "The page is printed." This also rules out that the writer guides the thought, so choice A is incorrect. Choice B is incorrect because the poem does not suggest that a writer must look to nature for inspiration, though the poem uses imagery and metaphor that involves nature. Choice C is incorrect because the fox represents the thought itself, rather than being a character or figure that assists the speaker in developing the thought or written work.

11. A: This poem was written in free verse, meaning it does not follow a metrical pattern, rhyme scheme, or particular poetic form, so choice A is correct. The poem is not in blank verse, which is poetry that follows a rhythm and metrical pattern but does not rhyme, so choice B is incorrect. Though the poem contains some rhymes, such as the eye rhyme of "snow" with "now," the slant rhyme of "star" with "near," and the rhyme of "snow" with "hollow," there is no regular rhyme scheme, so choice C is incorrect. The poem does not have a particular number of beats per line, so it is not metered, and choice D is incorrect.

12. B: The best model a teacher can provide to students in this situation is effective reading strategies that result in better overall comprehension. Choice B effectively accomplishes this by first reading for the main idea, which is easier to grasp than smaller details that can be misleading or unrelated to the point of the passage. Reading, then re-reading is a great skill to show students to help them know to approach the text and be willing to put more time in to understand the passage more fully, rather than just looking for information for a particular answer. Choice A is wrong because while learning to underline meaningful information in a passage is useful, going straight to the place where the answers are located does not help model the overall search for information. Choice C is wrong because it pertains to general test-taking tips and is not directly related to reading comprehension or use of textual evidence. Choice D is wrong because it models weak practices. It is generally not a good idea to complete an organizational framework until you are well-acquainted with a passage. The whole text should be read first, then when the overall idea is understood, someone can go back and fill in a story map.

13. A: When readers consider why an author wrote an informational text, determining author purpose gives them greater insight into the text, so choice A is correct. Choice B is incorrect because considering author purpose helps to develop rather than weaken critical reading skills. Choice C is incorrect because considering author purpose helps readers form expectations and engage more thoroughly with the text. Choice D is incorrect because considering purpose helps to engage the reader and allows for a stronger response, making the text more meaningful for the reader.

14. A: Metaphor is a form of figurative language where a comparison is made but no comparative language (such as "like" or "as") is used. The sentence in choice A likens the Great Depression to a heavy shroud, or covering. Since it appears to say the Great Depression was a heavy shroud—not merely like a heavy shroud—it makes an implicit comparison. Therefore, choice A is correct. Choice B uses literal language, so it is incorrect. Choice C is incorrect because it compares the effects of the Great Depression to a cloud using the word *like*, which is an explicit comparison. Choice D is incorrect because, while it uses personification to say that the year "saw", this is not the same as a metaphor.

15. A: Dangling participle. "Our neighborhood" was NOT growing up, we were. Corrections: "<u>When we were</u> growing up" OR "<u>we found</u> our neighborhood safe enough."

16. A: Letter–sound correspondence relies on the relationship between a spoken sound or group of sounds and the letters conventionally used in English to write them.

17. C: Mark Twain's book *Adventures of Huckleberry Finn* includes various Southern American dialects to enhance the reader's sense of the setting and characters, so choice C is correct. A dialect encompasses variations from the standard not only in vocabulary but in pronunciation and grammar as well. Choice A is incorrect because *jargon* refers only to vocabulary—specifically to a body of terms used and understood mainly by those in a particular field, profession, or hobby. Choice B is incorrect because the term *slang* also refers to vocabulary that is not considered Standard English but is used by particular age groups or subcultures. Choice D is incorrect because *accent* refers to a set of shifts in pronunciation; the term does not extend to the grammatical and lexical variations that make up a dialect.

18. A: Considering audience is not necessary in order to determine purpose, so choice A is correct. Choice B is incorrect because writers should use audience and purpose to decide on the best structure and organization for those who will read the writing. Choice C is incorrect, as audience, along with purpose of writing, will determine what style and tone to use in a piece of writing, and will therefore affect word choice. Identifying an audience will also help in choosing specific words that will be most understandable and appealing to readers. Finally, choice D is incorrect because audience will also dictate how much time to spend on research. Some readers will expect more supporting evidence, while others will not.

19. A: This version is correctly punctuated because it is a compound-complex sentence, consisting of two independent clauses and a dependent/subordinate (relative) clause. Independent clauses should be separated by a semicolon. In (B) and (D), the two independent clauses have no punctuation separating them, creating a run-on sentence; additionally, (B) has an incorrect comma between the first independent clause and the subordinating conjunction "that," which introduces the relative clause. (If "that" were omitted, it would be correct with or without the comma.) Version (C) incorrectly separates the independent clauses with a comma instead of a semicolon.

20. C: Signal words give the reader hints about the purpose of a particular passage. Some signal words are concerned with comparing/contrasting, some with cause and effect, some with temporal sequencing, some with physical location, and some with a problem and its solution. The words since, therefore, and accordingly are words used when describing an outcome; outcomes have causes.

21. B: Assessment is an ongoing process that involves formal testing and a host of other methods. Students are working at any given time in the school year on a multitude of skill sets, and all of these skills are interrelated and developing simultaneously at different rates. It is difficult to provide a complete "snapshot" of a student's abilities, because each student develops in a unique and complex manner. Choice A would only offer insight into a student's reading fluency. Choice C would show how a student could perform on standardized tests; however, many factors such as anxiety and test-taking speed affect those scores. Choice D relies on the teacher to interpret the student's strengths and weaknesses and would require an almost impossible attention to detail. Choice B includes both formal and informal assessments as well as giving insight into writing, vocabulary and other skill sets in a comprehensive portfolio.

22. D: This is an example of nonparallel structure. The first three verbs ("hiking, swimming, rowing") are gerunds (verb participles ending with *-ing,* used as nouns—in this sentence, they are direct objects). Then suddenly the fourth verb ("to climb mountains") is an infinitive. It does not match the others, creating a lack of parallel structure. The sentence should read either "hiking, swimming, rowing, and climbing mountains" or "to hike, to swim, to row, and to climb mountains"/ "to hike, swim, row, and climb mountains."

23. D: Finding correlations (A) requires considering the relationship between ideas or items. Making analogies (B) only considers similarities, while contrasting (C) only considers differences. Categorizing requires consideration of similarities in order to group items together and consideration of differences to ensure that the different groups are distinct from each other, making choice D correct.

24. D: An essay's introduction should always include the subject of the essay and what the essay is meant to prove. The essay's thesis statement is the sentence within the introduction that explains what the writer is attempting to prove by writing the essay. The introduction often also contains an essay map, which is a statement that briefly highlights some of the main ideas of the essay in the order that they will appear in the body of the essay. The purpose of an essay can be simple or difficult to determine. Sometimes the writer will explicitly state their purpose (motive) for writing an essay, but this is not always the case. Many essays require deeper analysis to determine the author's purpose. Although the author's purpose, essay subject, and thesis statement are usually aligned with each other, they are not the same thing. For example, an author who wants to increase tourism to America's National Parks might write an essay with the subject "America's National Parks" and the thesis statement "America's National Parks are fun, beautiful, and affordable vacation destinations."

25. B: While connecting texts with other texts can be useful, it is not required in order to understand, critically judge, draw conclusions about, and make personal interpretations of informational text. Therefore, choice B is correct. In order to understand, critically judge, draw conclusions about, and make their own interpretations of informational text, students must be able to locate evidence in the text (A), organize the information in the text, differentiate between main ideas and details in the text, make inferences about the text (C), and connect the text to their prior knowledge (D).

26. C: Strength and closure are important principles for written conclusions. Choice C is correct because word count does not necessarily mean the piece is complete. Although length is important and can affect the strength of a text as a whole, it does not affect the strength of a text's conclusion. Choice A is incorrect because a conclusion that highlights how the main points are meaningful and important reminds the reader why they should care about the text's topic, which provides good closure. Choice B is incorrect because a conclusion should include a statement that repeats the thesis or main argument that drove the rest of the piece. This, along with reiterating the main points and how they are connected, gives the author one final opportunity to express his or her message and succinctly illustrate that the message has been well supported. Choice D is incorrect because reinforcing the main points and reminding the reader how they are related is one of the crucial aspects of a text's conclusion and will assist readers in identifying and remembering the text's main points and supporting evidence.

27. D: When an online source is in the PDF file format or another file format that has stable pagination, MLA guidelines advise to include applicable page numbers in in-text citations because these numbers are valid and will not change. Therefore, choice D is correct. If an internet source has no pagination, as often happens, the MLA does not advise avoiding the citation, so choice A is incorrect. Rather, it advises simply making the citation without page numbers. Although a printout of an internet source will by necessity have page numbers (for the printed pages), these page numbers will be inconsistent from one printout to another, unlike PDFs. Therefore, the MLA advises not including these page numbers even if you see them, so choice B is incorrect. As already explained, there are cases where an online source will have stable pagination, and the MLA recommends including page numbers in citations of these sources, so choice C is incorrect.

28. A: In the word transcontinental, the prefix trans- means "across." A transcontinental railroad or flight goes across a continent. Choice B is incorrect because, although trans- can relate to change or transformation in words such as transform, that is not its meaning in transcontinental. Choice C is incorrect because carry comes from the root in words like transport, not from the prefix trans- itself. Choice D is incorrect because different is not a meaning of the prefix.

29. C: A simile is a literary device where *like* or *as* is used to figuratively compare one thing to another. The phrase *as light as a feather* in choice C is an example of this, so choice C is correct. The other choices are incorrect because the sentences in these choices contain metaphors. A metaphor is a literary device where a comparison is made for effect—just like in a simile—but neither *like* nor *as* is used. In other words, where a simile says that one thing is *like* another thing, a metaphor says that one thing really is another thing. For example, in choice A, nervousness is likened to a fluttering feeling in the stomach, but the sentence seems to say that Joe literally has butterflies in his stomach, instead of using *like* or *as* to clarify that it is merely a comparison.

30. B: Three nouns are included in the compound subject of this sentence, so the verb should be the plural "are," not the singular "is." There is only one verb, so any error of agreement between/among verb tenses (C) is impossible. Lack of parallel structure (D) involves disagreement among grammatical structures, e.g., "walking, running, and to jump" instead of "walking, running, and jumping." There is no such error in this sentence. Because (B) is correct, (A) is incorrect.

31. C: An informational text that explains one or more problems and how to solve those problems would follow a problem-solution text structure, so choice C is the correct answer. A process narrative structure would lay out a sequence of steps or stages. This structure would be more fitting for an informational text about how to write an essay rather than how to avoid errors commonly found in essays, so choice A is not the correct answer. Cause-and-effect structure organizes writing by whether the events being described are causes or effects. According to the question, the informational text would include some description of the effects of common writing mistakes. However, the whole text would not be organized based on these, so choice B is incorrect. Finally, a description uses sensory language, such as imagery, to help readers experience the subject of the writing. This structure would not be useful in listing common errors found in essays nor in explaining how to avoid these errors, so choice D is incorrect.

32. D: Informal Reading Inventories assess students in multiple areas of reading performance, including decoding, comprehension, recall, and fluency. The results can be used to identify areas in need of improvement, group students for targeted reading instruction, and match students with appropriate texts. They do not record texts students have read throughout the year, which can be done using reading logs, nor do they identify areas of student interest. Other assessment and screening tools exist to determine which reading behaviors and skills students have already learned prior to entering school.

33. C: Thinking about thinking, or understanding our own cognitive processes, is known as metacognition, so choice C is correct. Explicitly teaching effective reading comprehension strategies does more than deepen student understanding of reading. It also promotes the higher-order, abstract cognitive skill of metacognition. Choice A is not correct, as schemata are mental constructs we form to understand the world. Reading instructors may refer to experience or background knowledge as "schemata" because students fit what they read to their existing knowledge. Choice B is incorrect because scaffolding (in reading instruction) is temporary support that is given to students as needed while they learn and gradually reduced as the students become more independent. Educators may also describe students' connections of text to prior experience as scaffolding. Metamorphosis (D) is not relevant to reading instruction.

34. D: Choice D is correct because it reflects a ground rule that only warrants mention for younger children and children with behavioral disorders. The rule prohibits physically aggressive behaviors that are not common among older, typically developing children. The other choices are incorrect because they show rules that students' attention must be drawn to regardless of age or developmental level. These include no cross-talk (A), no interrupting others (B), and no monopolizing the discussion (C).

35. A: It is a standard of Information Literacy that students must use their own critical thinking skills to evaluate the quality of the information and its sources before they use it, so choice A is correct. Another standard of Information Literacy is that the student should ascertain how much information he or she needs before seeking out the information, as identifying what information is necessary after uncovering excessive information is inefficient (B). Instead of acquiring as much information as possible, students should determine how much information is needed to achieve a reasonable goal. An additional Information Literacy standard is to access necessary information in an efficient and effective way. However, none of these standards include the idea that students will sacrifice any incidental learning by being efficient in their accessing of information, so choice C is incorrect. Another part of Information Literacy Standards is the principle that students should use the information they find in ways that are effective for their specific purposes; this does not require that students avoid using information for purposes that it was not meant to serve, so choice D is incorrect.

36. B: The sentence is choice B appeals to the reader's emotions by stating simply that it is "really stupid" to use a cell phone while driving; it does not provide any evidence or logic to support the statement but relies on the emotion behind calling something stupid. Thus, choice B is correct. That steering one-handed makes driving more dangerous is a logical, common-sense argument, so choice A cannot be considered purely an appeal to emotion and is incorrect. Supporting evidence such as statistics is an appeal to logic, so choice C is incorrect. Citing the fact that many laws ban the use of cell phones while driving appeals to logic in that it supports the idea that this behavior is dangerous, and it appeals to authority in that it borrows some credibility from government. It is also not an appeal to emotion, so choice D is incorrect.

37. D: With digital media, teachers and students alike can use cross-media transformations to convert speech to text and text to speech, including automatically by embedding speech-to-text and text-to-speech software into browsers and other software programs. Choices A, B, and C are all advantages for diverse students that can be accomplished using HTML and/or XML to change or select fonts and make similar text choices.

38. A: Formative assessments are given during a unit of study to identify students' existing knowledge and gaps. They are used to guide instruction by helping a teacher determine if current instructional strategies are successful or if changes need to be made. Summative assessments are given at the end of a unit or after another extended period of time. Norm-referenced tests are standardized tests that compare students' performances to sample groups of similar students. Screening assessments are used to identify students who may be at risk for future academic difficulties and may benefit from interventions.

39. D: There are four main components to an effective outline. Subordination means that the information in the heading is more general, while the subheadings are more specific. For example:

I. Visit and Evaluate College Websites

A. Note important statistics

B. Look for interesting classes

The other three components of an effective outline include parallelism, coordination, and division.

40. C: Denotation is the literal meaning or dictionary definition of a word. Connotation is the figurative meaning of a word, including emotional or perceptual associations associated with the word but not included in its literal definition. The words "politician" and "statesman" have the same literal meaning or denotation. However, when used in context, "politician" may have either a neutral or negative connotation, whereas "statesman" usually has a positive connotation.

41. B: In most cases, it is best to write the introduction last. Although it is the first part of the finished work, the introduction provides a synopsis for what is in the entire document. Until the writing is complete, the writer cannot reflect on the work as a whole. Writing the introduction prior to the body runs the risk that what follows may not completely conform to the ideas expressed in the introduction. An introduction usually should not reinforce ideas made in the piece, as the body portion of a work is the best place to flesh out ideas. Answer D is incorrect because an introduction frames the rest of the work; it is an incorrect generalization that the introduction, body, or conclusion are always the most or least important parts.

42. B: The active reading strategy called text coding has nothing to do with writing computer code (a). Text monitoring is a synonym for text coding rather than a name for a different strategy (c). The authors cited recommend that, for students to perform text coding, teachers should model it for them (d) one or two codes at a time until students have learned all of the codes.

43. B: Mood refers to the emotions evoked in the reader by the literary work, whereas tone refers to the emotions or attitude of the author toward the subject matter or audience, making choice B correct. Choice C is the reverse of this, so it is not correct. Choice A is incorrect because mood and tone do not mean the same thing. Though mood and tone have different meanings, neither one is associated with particular techniques; the same literary techniques could be used for either purpose, so choice D is incorrect.

44. C: This is a complex sentence. It has one independent clause ("He could not finish the test in time") and a dependent clause ("even though he tried his hardest"), which is subordinate to and depends on the independent clause. It is not a compound–complex (A) sentence, which would have two independent clauses and at least one dependent clause, because it has only one independent clause. It is not a compound (B) sentence, which has at least two independent clauses but no dependent clauses, because it has only one independent clause and does include a dependent clause. It is not a simple (D) sentence, which would be only one independent clause with no dependent clause.

45. D: Explaining a process to readers (A), articulating a concept for readers (B), and presenting new information to readers (C) are all primary functions of informative or explanatory writing. Proving a point to convince readers to agree with the author's position (D) is a primary function of argumentative writing.

46. A: An allusion is a reference to something or someone well-known that adds symbolism and/or resonance. A paradox (B) is a seemingly contradictory statement which nevertheless is true. An analogy (C) is a comparison of two different things that share some common elements. A parody (D) is a kind of satire that ridicules a work's subject and/or style through imitation.

47. B: A maze test is a specific type of cloze test. In a cloze test, words are deleted, and the reader must supply the missing words using contextual clues and vocabulary that is familiar. A maze test is essentially a multiple-choice application of a cloze test.

48. D: *Onomatopoeia* refers to words that sound like the sound they represent when spoken aloud. For example, the sound of the word *hum* resembles the sound humming makes. Likewise, *click*, when pronounced, sounds like a click, and *buzz* sounds like buzzing. Although *moan* does refer to a sound, the word is not derived from the sound of moaning. Therefore, choice D is correct.

49. A: Choices B, C, and D use literal meaning by factually describing the willow's appearance. Though the language is descriptive, it deals with physical shape and appearance and does not involve comparisons that suggest deeper ideas about the tree's character or the emotions it might evoke. Choice A uses figurative language with the metaphor of "weeping," which goes beyond physical description and suggests that the tree has a sadness about it. Choice A also uses personification by attributing human abilities to the nonhuman willow.

50. A: *The Adventures of Huckleberry Finn* by Mark Twain is a novel. *The Diary of a Young Girl* by Anne Frank is a non-fictional journal. "The Fall of the House of Usher" by Edgar Allan Poe is a fictional short story. Novels, personal narratives (e.g., diaries and journals), and short stories are all examples of narrative writing. Therefore choice A is correct. The events described in *Huckleberry Finn* and "The Fall of the House of Usher" do not correspond to real-life events, so choice B is incorrect. Choice C is incorrect as none of the works were ever considered to be a radical social commentary, though *Huckleberry Finn* and *The Diary of a Young Girl* have been banned by various countries or institutions for various reasons. All three of the works are written in the first-person narrative viewpoint, so choice D is incorrect.

51. A: A work written in the second-person refers to the reader or listener as *you*. Second person also includes the usage of an implied subject, which is the understood *you*. This is rarely used in literary works such as novels, so choice A is correct. The second-person viewpoint is more frequently used in song lyrics, advertisements, and instruction manuals.

52. C: When students quote others' writing in their research papers, it is important to follow each quotation with an explanation, interpretation, or summary that clarifies its relevance to their argument. This ensures that the quotation is integrated meaningfully rather than left standing alone. (C) correctly reflects this principle. (A) is incorrect because citing studies parenthetically does not interrupt an argument if done properly. (B) is incorrect because word count relative to a quotation does not determine padding. (D) is incorrect because summarizing content is less original and engaging than analysis, synthesis, or evaluation.

53. C: Choice C is correct because reporting findings from case studies is a rhetorical means of providing evidence to support purposes, viewpoints, or claims in informational text. Choice A is incorrect because relating personal anecdotes is a rhetorical means of appealing to reader emotions and making points more relatable or accessible to readers, but not of providing evidence. Choice B is incorrect because making analogies to clarify ideas is a rhetorical means of explaining by helping readers connect ideas in the text to knowledge they already have. Choice D is incorrect because laying out premises and conclusions provides a logical argument based on deductive reasoning, but it does not provide evidence.

54. C: The statement "And even the name of the legendary King Arthur" is not a complete sentence and thus cannot stand on its own. The period that is placed before the word *And* should be removed and the two statements combined.

55. D: Credibility is related to how believable readers felt the author's writing was, which is a major element of whether the author's appeals changed the readers' minds. Clarity, another criterion for evaluating methods of appeal, is related to how clearly the author presented the content. Accuracy, an additional criterion, is related to whether the content that the author included was factually correct. Cohesion, also an evaluative criterion, has to do with how well the author's arguments and appeals are connected and related to one another, which helps readers understand them and holds their interest.

56. B: Suffixes appear at the end of words, while prefixes appear at the beginning of words.

57. C: Evaluating arguments used in informational text involves several elements. One element is to test if all the premises and the conclusion of an argument are true. Choice C accurately states this, so it is the correct answer. The other answers refer to actions the reader must take, but they explain these actions incorrectly. Readers should identify not only the assumptions that the author has stated, but also the assumptions the author has implied but omitted, so choice A is incorrect. Choice B is incorrect because readers should word unstated assumptions sympathetically from what they perceive as the author's perspective. Choice D is incorrect because, for arguments using inductive reasoning, readers should test how strongly all of the true premises support the conclusion, not check whether the argument is valid or invalid, which would apply to deductive reasoning.

58. B: The primary purpose of visual aids is to extend or enhance meaning. Visuals can sometimes distract from the meaning of the presentation if used too much, as in Choice A. Choice C could also create distractions in that students may be more likely to look at photos directly in front of them than pay attention to the student presenting. The final choice simply encourages students to read the information on screen, and will likely cause the presenting student to read aloud rather than communicate in his own words. Choice B, however, utilizes the students' thought processes in determining where a visual might help enhance understanding, and requires them to use oral communication as well.

59. B: Main characters are usually dynamic, meaning they change throughout the story. Generally, these changes result from one or more conflicts in the story and how the character responds to them. Choice A is incorrect because static characters are characters who are not developed throughout the story, whereas dynamic characters are well-developed. Choice C is incorrect because round characters are ones that have complex and changeable traits. A character who does not go through any development in a story is a static character. Choice D is incorrect because authors use foils to make a main character's traits more obvious, not less obvious.

60. C: Choice C is correct because both TV and radio can raise awareness, interest, and excitement. Choice A is incorrect because both TV and radio are high-status mass media (i.e., they reach many people). Choice B is incorrect, as TV has a broad reach and radio has a broad-to-medium reach. Choice D is incorrect because, while TV enables messages to be targeted for certain audiences, radio works better for specific audiences, such as people who listen to a particular local station every day.

61. B: Choice B is correct, because paragraphs that are underdeveloped are by definition unconvincing and ineffective. Choice A is incorrect because another failing of underdeveloped paragraphs (and one of the reasons they are said to be underdeveloped) is that they do not always provide needed background. Choice C is incorrect because such paragraphs may still be well-written in some sense. Choice D is incorrect because underdeveloped paragraphs may include some required information, though they characteristically do not provide all of it.

62. A: Choice A includes a description of the student's appearance and a brief piece of dialogue. A person's face becoming pale often indicates that the person is sick, nervous, or afraid. The dialogue shows that the students were not able to complete a test, which is likely to have negative consequences. This sentence contains implicit meaning, as the physical description implies that the student is distressed by the possible consequences of failing to complete the test. Choice B explicitly states the students' emotional state and the reason for it. Choice C explicitly states that the students could not complete the test and does not include any details to be interpreted. Choice D explicitly states the students' shared emotion, external sign of this emotion, and the reason they feel this way.

63. C: Sample 1's author cites evidence that is tangential to his argument, hence it is not relevant. Sample 2's author cites anecdotal evidence which is inaccurate, hence it is not factual. Sample 3's author cites evidence which is factual (accurate) and relevant (directly related), but not sufficient (an isolated example uncorroborated by any other sources). Criteria for evaluating evidence used in informational text include that the evidence be relevant, factual, and sufficient to accomplish the author's purpose (for example, proving the author's point or points and/or persuading the reader).

64. B: The green light in *The Great Gatsby* is a famous example of symbolism. In the novel, the green light symbolizes unattainable desires. For Gatsby, the light is closely connected to Daisy. The narrator suggests Gatsby's desire for Daisy is more satisfying for Gatsby than Daisy herself seems to be, so rather than representing love, the green light seems to symbolize desires that cannot be attained, or desire itself. Choice A is incorrect; though a fateful love affair does take place, nothing about the green light suggests this to the reader. Choice C is also incorrect. While the green color of the light connects to a theme of wealth in the novel, and the green light itself is often regarded as a symbol of the American Dream, Gatsby has already attained a level of considerable wealth, so such a metaphor would not apply to him. Choice D is incorrect because there is not necessarily any distance between Gatsby and Daisy, who have an affair and live near one another. On the other hand, the location of the light highlights the figurative distance between Gatsby and his desires.

65. A: When a speaker is making a statement or answering a question from the audience, s/he should not take three or more minutes to get to the point, which will lose listener attention. Getting off the subject has the same effect. However, speakers should not be afraid to pause before answering audience questions (B): this gives them time to formulate a clear response, as well as demonstrating to their listeners that they are thoughtful and in control. Including too many anecdotes and details (C) is not good: it causes audiences to lose track of the subject/get confused. Similarly, speakers should include necessary information but not all other interesting information. (D): Information overload triggers listeners' brains to shut down due to having more input than they can process.

66. C: The sentence in choice C is most likely to be the topic sentence of a supporting paragraph, as it begins with a transition word that suggests it is the last point among several, but also suggests that there will be a few points (or "consequences") that show why excessive carbon emission is a threat. The sentence in choice A uses "it" to refer to an earlier noun, which is not effective in a topic sentence. Choice B seems likely to be a summary or plan of development, as lists points that seem likely to be explained in more detail. Choice D extends a thought to the reader's life, so it would most likely serve as a lesson in a concluding paragraph.

67. B: This sentence has two independent clauses. Because they are independent clauses, they must be either separated with a period or semicolon or connected with a comma and a coordinating conjunction. With adverbs that tend to serve as transitions (such as "moreover"), a common pattern is to use a semicolon to separate the clauses, and then place the adverb with a comma before the second clause as in choice B: "Not all permission slips were returned; moreover, the bus was unavailable." Choices A and D are examples of common errors related to this pattern. Choice C is more obviously incorrect, with a semicolon separating "moreover" from the clause that it modifies.

68. D: With possessive pronouns, do not use an apostrophe. *You're* and *it's* are contractions of *you are* and *it is* respectively. *Your nametag* and *its place* are correct, so choice D is the right answer. Choice A incorrectly adds an apostrophe to both possessive adjectives. Choice B uses *your* correctly, but *it's* is incorrect. Choice C uses *you're* incorrectly but *its* correctly.

69. A: Rubrics are a type of evaluation tool that assign both overall scores and scores in individual component areas of an assignment. In each component area, the criteria used to assign scores for different levels of mastery are outlined. Therefore, students can see their overall grades on assignments, as well as how they performed in each component area. This helps students assess their strengths and weaknesses. Rubrics do not specifically track progress over time, though teachers could evaluate students using the same rubric at different points of the year and compare the results. Rubrics assess individual performance and do not compare students to their peers. Choice D describes a miscue analysis, which is a different type of assessment.

70. B: Because the tabletop is the largest and most conspicuous part of a table, it corresponds, in this analogy, with the main idea of an essay or other written composition. Because the legs support the table, they represent the evidence and details that support the top or main idea—not vice versa, so choice A is incorrect. Neither the table's legs nor the tabletop represents individual paragraphs, so choices C and D are incorrect.

71. A: Choice A is correct because it most accurately reflects research from the National Reading Technical Assistance Center (NRTAC). In 2010, NRTAC found that because children often must learn specific word meanings to understand texts, lessons, or subjects, teachers must provide direct instruction on the vocabulary words involved. To retain newly acquired vocabulary words, students need repeated exposure in varied contexts, not drilling, so choice B is incorrect. To increase productive language skills, students need to be taught high-frequency words so that they can apply them in many contexts, so choice C is incorrect. When students understand task expectations, they frequently learn faster; hence teachers should restructure vocabulary exercises as needed and choice D is incorrect.

72. C: Longer sentences are not necessarily clauses. A clause must have a subject and a finite verb. Choice C has no verb, so it is the correct answer. Choices A and B both contain clauses, so they are not correct. Choice D is also a clause, so it is incorrect. Note that it is possible to introduce a complete sentence with *then*, because it is an adverb, not a subordinating conjunction or a relative pronoun.

73. A: "However" is an adverb when it is used to modify a whole clause, as it is in this sentence, making choice A correct. A pronoun is a generalized word (such as he or she) that can substitute for more specific nouns when the listener or reader will know which noun is being referred to. "However" isn't referring to another noun, so choice B is incorrect. A preposition connects nouns, pronouns, noun phrases, and pronoun phrases to other words; in this sentence, *to* and *with* are prepositions. Since "however" is not connecting phrases to each other, choice C is incorrect. Although "however" can act as a conjunction, this is only the case when it means "in whatever way that," as in the sentence "However you do it, just get it done." This meaning is not the one used in the question, so choice D is incorrect.

74. B: These are examples of grouping animals into categories. Authors connect and distinguish ideas and things in informational texts by making analogies, like "a frog is to an insect as a lion is to an antelope"—in other words, predator to prey. Another example includes comparing their similarities and/or contrasting their differences. For instance, some animals have simple life cycles; others, like frogs, undergo metamorphosis; and some insects undergo complete metamorphosis including egg, larval, pupal, and adult stages, while other insects, like grasshoppers, dragonflies, and cockroaches undergo incomplete metamorphosis with egg, nymph, and adult stages but no pupal stage.

75. A: Generally, if a story is told by one of its characters and from the character's own perspective (using "I" when referring to the narrating character), the point of view is first person (A). In second-person point of view (B), the written story addresses the reader and involves them in the story using the word "you." Limited third-person point of view (C) is like a "fly on the wall" narration, where the narrator is not a character in the story, but they have a perspective that is akin to a character within the story, so their perspective is limited. In omniscient third-person point of view (D), the narrator knows everything, including the thoughts and feelings of the characters.

76. D: While a beginning writer may sometimes regard the conclusion of their essay or paper as simply the last paragraph and therefore include any information and or points that they want to present but cannot fit elsewhere, the conclusion is not meant for this purpose, so choice D is the correct answer. The true purposes of the conclusion are to summarize the main body of the essay (A), to recall or echo the thesis statement (C), and to clarify the context or application of the essay content (B), as by providing a lesson or extended thought. Therefore, choices A, B, and C are incorrect.

77. A: Research papers on English language and literature topics are generally expected to use the Modern Language Association (MLA) style, so choice A is correct. The other choices are styles that research papers may be required or expected to follow but that are not standard for English-related topics. Research papers in psychology, sociology, or other social sciences are usually expected to use American Psychological Association (APA) style. The Chicago style, which is defined in *The Chicago Manual of Style*, may be preferred by specific institutions or instructors across subjects, but it is also not the standard for research papers in English-related topics. American Medical Association (AMA) style is a standard requirement for research papers in health and medicine, but not in English-related topics.

78. C: By using varied books for read-alouds and shared reading activities, the teacher can ensure that students are exposed to a variety of genres and text structures. During these activities, the teacher can also help students explore the features of these texts. Choice A can be used to support this instruction, but the posters alone are not as likely to be effective as actually exploring varied types of books. Choices B and D do not ensure that all students will actually explore different types of texts.

79. D: Personification is a metaphor in which a thing or abstraction is represented as a person. Personification is used to varying degrees throughout the poem, but of the answer choices given, the one that represents Spring as a woman waking from sleep is the best example.

80. D: Choices A, B, and C all refer to printed sources. Citations for print sources generally do not need to include access dates because the content of the source will not change. Even if new editions are printed that include important differences, the edition and date of publication will already be present in the citation so readers will know which edition of the source the author is referencing. Online sources, on the other hand, often do require a date of access in their citation because the content of many online sources can change over time, so choice D is correct.

81. C: Among the choices, only choice C seems unlikely to be helpful in character analysis. In order to understand a literary character and analyze his or her development, readers should keep a few things in mind. One element to pay close attention to is the observations the narrator makes about a character, as the author likely has a reason for including these in the work (A). The reader can also observe contradictions in what a character thinks, says, and does, as these may reveal internal conflict and may play a role in the character's development (B). Additionally, readers can note differences between how the other characters in the story talk about a character and how the narrator talks about the character. This can reveal facts about the character's relationships with other characters, for example, and reveal how aware a character is of their own behavior or qualities.

82. A: Millay's meaning, in more ordinary syntax, is "all that I was once" (or "all that I once was"). She did not mean "once I was all that," "that I once all was," or "that all I was once." These either mean something different or do not make sense. She makes her syntax more unusual and poetic—first by placing the adverb *once* ahead of the subject and verb, and second by reversing the usual order of subject + verb, "I was" to verb + subject, "was I."

83. D: Epigrams are composed of one to a few lines of poetry designed to be memorable because of their cleverness, word choice, and brevity. An example is Benjamin Franklin's "Early to bed and early to rise/Makes a man healthy, wealthy, and wise." Odes (A), very popular during the Romantic period, are typically complex and can be lengthy. Epics (B) are long poems telling of adventures and heroic accomplishments. In English language poetry, elegies (C) are poems that lament a death or other sad event.

84. B: Choice B uses *greasy* in a nonliteral way; it does not mean that the smile is covered in grease, but that smile has a quality one might call *greasy* with a negative connotation. While *heavy* can be used with different connotations, when describing a desk, it is likely intended to have the denotative meaning, so choice A is not correct. Likewise, *blue* in choice C and *formal* in choice D use denotative meanings to give objective descriptions.

85. A: When students write the concluding paragraphs of their essays and they restate their main thesis, it is better to paraphrase it rather than to repeat the same thesis statement from the essay's introduction word for word. Teachers should advise students NOT to apologize for the opinions they expressed or their writing technique in essay conclusions. They should also instruct students that it is NOT necessary for them to use their conclusions to summarize the essay every single time.

86. D: The student has used the same adjective, "wonderful," four times in the same sentence to modify four different nouns. To give her description more variety, she should consult an online thesaurus to find synonyms (e.g., terrific, great, outstanding, exemplary, etc.). A grammar guide (a) will not offer vocabulary synonyms, and the student's sentence has no grammatical issues. An encyclopedia (b) offers information on many subjects, but not word synonyms. An online dictionary (c) will provide a few to several synonyms for "wonderful," but a thesaurus will offer many more.

87. B: All four authors wrote novels and short stories in the 19th century. While O. Henry (A) is perhaps better known for his short stories, Herman Melville (C) and Nathaniel Hawthorne (D) are best known for their novels. All three were American authors. Charles Dickens (B), who wrote many famous novels as well as short stories, is the only British author among these four.

88. C: One theme in the play is that of fate and the fact that it does control the characters, who are referred to as "star-crossed lovers," so choice A is not correct. Shakespeare does not attribute the tragedy in the play to the characters' youth (B). Though love does compel characters in the play to ignore certain realities, neither Romeo nor Juliet is blissfully blind to any personal flaws in the other (D). Only choice C is an accurate summary of one theme of the play, that crossing certain social boundaries can lead to violence and death.

89. B: The author sending his proposal to turn his book into a movie would be the first step. In the second step, one or more parties would turn the proposal into a more detailed story line. This is called a treatment, and it's much more substantive than a proposal and much less substantive than a screenplay, or script. The third step in the process is for the producer to sell the idea to a movie studio. Once they give him the green light, the last step before production begins is writing a script, or screenplay. In most cases, this will not be done by the author of the book.

90. A: From the syntax of this sentence, the reader can determine which parts of speech the missing words must be: the first blank must be filled by a noun, the second by a verb. However, the reader cannot determine from syntax which specific noun or verb these should be (B). The noun must be a thing, place, or event, but this encompasses a great many words (e.g., building, site, meeting, party, riot, class, school, company, etc.). The verb must be transitive because it takes an object ("what happened"), but this also includes myriad verbs (e.g., see, observe, find out, discover, report, address, change, correct, imitate, avoid, etc.). Therefore, answers (C) and (D) are incorrect.

91. D: This is an example of a compound-complex sentence, so choice D is correct. The other choices are incorrect, as they refer to different sentence types. A simple (A) sentence contains no more than one independent clause (i.e., a subject and a finite verb) and no dependent clauses. Its subject and verb may be compound (e.g., "John and Mary" as the subject, or "comes and goes" as the verb). A complex (B) sentence contains an independent clause and one or more dependent clauses.

Dependent clauses are joined to independent clauses or other dependent clauses by subordinating conjunctions (as in "after she left") or relative pronouns (as in "that he had never heard"). A compound (C) sentence contains two or more independent clauses. The compound-complex sentence, as its name implies, combines both compound and complex sentence structures. It combines more than one independent clause with at least one dependent clause. In the example sentence given, the first two clauses, joined by "however," are independent, and the clause modifying "actual test questions," beginning with "which cover," is a relative, dependent clause.

92. C: According to research from the National Institute of Child Health and Human Development (NICHD, 2000), receptive comprehension vs. expressive production (A), written and printed vocabulary vs. spoken vocabulary (B), and vocabulary depth vs. breadth (D) are all aspects of vocabulary instruction and learning needing further investigation. However, researchers already widely agree without calling for additional study that students must learn not only word definitions, but moreover how words function in different contexts (C).

93. B: From the description of her appearance, her approach to love, and the companions in her life, readers can infer that Mamzelle Aurélie relies on herself, but also that she is set in her ways and likes to be in charge. Therefore, choice B is correct. Though she seems to have certain personal virtues, such as discipline and independence, nothing in the passage suggests she is naïve, so choice A is incorrect. Having declined a marriage proposal suggests she has attracted suitors. Her lack of regret for declining the proposal shows that she is not trying to attract suitors and is not lonely, so choice C does not make sense. Nothing in the passage suggests that she is cruel or emotionless, so choice D is incorrect.

94. B: The text in Choice B, along with the title of the story and the opening of the second paragraph, suggests to the reader that Mamzelle Aurélie will likely either get married or regret not getting married. Although choice A might lead the reader to make an inference that the coat and hat belonged to a male friend or relative who was important to her, it does not hint at any events that will occur later in the story. Choice C may cause readers to speculate about the significance of Ponto, but it does not clearly suggest later changes. Similarly, Choice D does not suggest any specific changes that will take place later, though the reader may wonder if the gun has any significance to the plot.

95. C: Choice C is correct, because in this passage, the reader gets a strong sense that Mamzelle Aurélie has everything just the way she likes it and does not need or want anyone else to depend on. However, the lack of other people in Mamzelle Aurélie's life is emphasized, and the notion that she will come to regret something is foreshadowed. Choice A is incorrect because it generalizes Mamzelle Aurélie's situation to all single women, but the passage only focuses on the peculiarities of Mamzelle Aurélie's life. Choice B is incorrect because it makes conclusions based on a supporting detail rather than a main idea. Choice D is incorrect because the passage foreshadows imminent regret, not the relief of regret.

96. D: Choice A, the suffix *-ation,* commonly forms nouns from verbs (e.g., *converse* and *conversation*, *confront* and *confrontation).* Choice B, the suffix *-ness,* commonly forms nouns from adjectives (e.g., *happy* and *happiness*). Choice C, the suffix *-ity,* also commonly forms nouns from adjectives (e.g., *formal* and *formality*, *sensitive* and *sensitivity).* Choice D, the suffix *-al*, can be used to form both nouns and adjectives from another part of speech. It is often used to form adjectives from nouns (e.g., *exception* and *exceptional*, *nation* and *national*) and nouns from verbs (e.g., *refuse* and *refusal*, *arrive* and *arrival*).

97. C: Evidence-based instructional approaches are proven via multiple rigorous research studies sharing consistent results. Choice C is correct because student outcomes should be evaluated using appropriate, established measures. Choice A is incorrect because the teaching practices should be defined in advance in order to evaluate the effectiveness of approaches. Choice B is incorrect because evaluators should establish a monitoring process to assure compliance. Choice D is incorrect because student progress with a specific teaching method should be compared to their progress without that method via suitable means.

98. C: Speculation, by its open-ended nature, explores possibilities and stimulates questions rather than asserting answers, so it does not make as clear or definitive points as exposition or argument. Therefore, choice C is correct. Choice A is incorrect because speculative writing does not aim to inform or direct readers as expository writing does, nor to persuade readers as argumentative writing does. Choice B is incorrect because, while speculative writing is less factual than exposition, it is typically more imaginative than argumentation or persuasion. Consistent with its nature, speculative writing tends to use looser structures than the other two forms of writing in the question, so choice D is incorrect.

99. B: Among the possible answers, choice B is the best definition of paragraph cohesion, because cohesion involves supporting details all relating to a main point and fitting together well. Solid evidence is helpful for making a point (A), but this is not an important aspect of paragraph cohesion. Paragraphs should begin with topic sentences, but they do not need to end with closing sentences, and having a topic sentence and a closing sentence does not by itself equate to paragraph cohesion (C). Likewise, appropriate transition words are important for cohesion (D), but they do not automatically make a paragraph cohesive.

100. B: A semicolon is used to punctuate between two independent clauses, as in the sentence given. It is also used in sentences that contain additional internal punctuation, which this sentence also has. (A) is incorrect because it contains a comma splice, i.e., two independent clauses joined by a comma without a coordinating conjunction (such as "and" or "but"). (C) is not as correct because it separates two related clauses with a period; joining them with a semicolon reinforces their connection. Choice (D) incorrectly uses a semicolon together with the coordinating conjunction "and." With a coordinating conjunction between independent clauses, a comma should be used rather than a semicolon.

101. A: A complex sentence combines independent and dependent clauses. The first clause is independent, the second ("although...") is dependent as it cannot stand alone as a sentence. Choice (B) is a compound sentence (i.e., two independent clauses joined by a semicolon and a conjunctive adverb). Choice (C) is a simple sentence (i.e., a single independent clause). Choice (D) is a compound–complex sentence (i.e., two independent clauses joined by coordinating conjunction ("and"), followed by a dependent ("if ...") clause).

102. B: The teacher used an informal reading inventory to gain insight into the students' abilities in a larger group setting. While some informal reading inventories, or IRIs, are administered between one teacher and one student, these inventories usually work best in a group setting. The benefit of this type of assessment is that it provides insight within the context of an entire class or large group in a short period of time. This assessment does not provide specific or generalized information about the students' progress, but rather allows the teacher to gauge her students' needs at any given point during instruction.

103. D: For the vast majority of people attending a presentation in a foreign country, English will not be their native language, and many of them will struggle to keep up with a presentation in

English, so it should not be complex, or very long. It would be wise to include, not avoid, anecdotes from the country, and quotes from nationals. American idioms should be avoided, as idioms by their nature do not translate well.

104. A: When evaluating the strength of an analysis that is based on textual evidence, we do not need to consider whether the analysis explains the author's intended meaning or purpose, so choice A is correct. The other choices are incorrect because they refer to considerations that are relevant when evaluating the strength of a prediction. Criteria for such an evaluation include standards for the evidence and standards for the analysis. The best possible evidence is strong (i.e., convincing), relevant, and accurate (B). Evidence should be specific, and it should be included in the analysis as a paraphrase or a direct quote (C). The best possible analysis shows special insight into a theme, character, or story event (D).

105. A: Lack of parallelism. Corrections: "to stay at home, cook dinner, and *watch* TV" OR "*staying* at home, *cooking* dinner, and watching TV."

106. B: The student used the present-tense verb forms go instead of went and have instead of had in describing actions that took place in the past. The student also used the idiomatically incorrect preposition on instead of in. The student did not make any other errors.

107. B: Students predicting what will happen in a text helps to support active reading by creating expectations for the text and the desire to see these expectations met (A). Summarizing current knowledge can activate what students already know, which can lead to better engagement because students may see the opportunity to learn more (C). Looking ahead and coming up with questions the text may answer combines these two concepts, prompting students to form expectations and identify what they hope to learn (D). Drawing a story map after reading is useful, but drawing one of predictions made before reading would go into too much depth about ideas that may not even be in the text. This is least likely to be effective in supporting active reading, making choice B correct.

108. B: "Nancy also felt that the party was too crowded" is an independent clause because it has a subject ("Nancy"), verb ("felt"), and could stand alone as a complete sentence. "The hosts would have been hurt" is also an independent clause. These two independent clauses are joined by the coordinating conjunction "but." "Who relied so much on her" is a dependent clause modifying the subject of the second independent clause, "the hosts." "If she had not attended" is an adjectival dependent clause, introduced by the subordinating conjunction "if" and modifying the predicate "would have been hurt" in the second independent clause. "That the party was too crowded" is an adverbial dependent clause, introduced by the subordinating conjunction "that" and modifying the verb "felt."

109. C: The rhyme scheme of this stanza is AABB; the first and second lines rhyme with each other ("love" and "prove"), and the third and fourth lines rhyme with each other ("fields" and "yields"). This use of rhyming couplets was popular in the poetry of the time.

110. A: Repetition—of words, phrases, sounds, images, or ideas—and appeal to sentiment are both effective tools of persuasion. Repetition causes consumers to better recall information, regardless of their response to the message itself. Appeal to sentiment taps into consumers' emotions, making consumers more likely to engage with the content. Choice B is incorrect because "weasel words" that qualify claims tend to be needed for overstated claims rather than understated ones. Choice C is incorrect because advertising uses humor to persuade more often than news or advocacy. Choice D is incorrect because hyperbole, superlatives, and intensifiers are used frequently across the advertising world and do not reflect anything about the quality of the advertising content in which they are used.

111. A: News articles published on the internet are more formal in their content and language than blogs (B), which are written from a more personal, less journalistic perspective. News articles are also more formal than emails (C), which can be even more casual than blogs as they involve communications between individuals rather than writing intended for larger audiences like blogs and news articles. Hence, these are not all the same in formality level (D).

112. C: Naturalism is a type of realistic fiction. The Naturalist movement took place in France, America, and England in the late 19th and early 20th centuries. Naturalists believed that people were controlled by both outer and inner forces.

113. A: A soliloquy is a speech made by one character in a play speaking alone, as opposed to dialogue between/among multiple characters. Some poets (e.g., Robert Browning) have written entire poems in the voice of a single character; however, these are called dramatic monologues rather than soliloquies, a term generally reserved for drama, not poetry (B). Similarly, in novels (C), conversation between/among characters is called dialogue, whereas a long speech by one character would be called a monologue. Essays (D) are typically nonfiction and do not contain characters or their speech.

114. A: Both books are diaries of 20th-century teenage girls. However, while Beatrice Sparks created a fictional plot and characters in her novel using diary format, Anne Frank's diary is nonfiction, written by a real person (B). The fictional Alice develops a somewhat negative perspective on life through her experiences (e.g., she is left with permanent neurological damage), she returns home and hopes for a better life. Anne Frank's entries, on the other hand, convey a markedly positive attitude despite horrific realities (C). The fictional Alice survives; following Frank's last, optimistic entry, an epilogue reports her death soon after (D).

115. C: Mnemonic devices help with remembering key sets of information by organizing it into patterns. For example, many mnemonic devices are made by identifying a series of initial letters corresponding to the words that must be remembered but forming an easily remembered acronym or phrase using the same initial letters (such as "RAFT" or "Role, Audience, Format, Topic" to help students remember the key elements of a writing assignment). The other answer choices reflect devices that are useful for reading and writing but are not specifically used for remembering key sets of information. Making outlines (A) helps with identifying main ideas and supporting details and organizing them into a hierarchy. Checklists (B) help ensure one has completed all steps or components of a task or project. Graphic organizers (D) help with visually representing abstract concepts and relationships.

116. B: Although passive voice is widely discouraged today, it can sometimes facilitate paragraph cohesion. The passive voice may allow information to presented in a more logical flow. Consider "Specialized teams worked to recover artwork stolen by the Third Reich, but many priceless pieces were lost nevertheless" compared to "Specialized teams worked to recover artwork stolen by the Third Reich, but the world nevertheless lost many priceless pieces from these collections." The passive voice may also provide writers with additional options for arranging words and ideas where active voice would be awkward or distracting. Consider "The Pyramids were built between 2000 and 3000 BC" compared to "Egyptians built the Pyramids between 2000 and 3000 BC." Therefore, passive voice can be useful for paragraph cohesion, and choice B is correct. As demonstrated above, the passive voice does not automatically make paragraphs less cohesive, so choice A is incorrect. Clearly the passive voice is not critical for cohesion, so choice C is also incorrect. Finally, choice D is incorrect because it is too extreme; the passive voice can be used effectively in many situations, not only when it is needed.

117. D: The author of this poem, Emily Dickinson, uses personification by attributing human qualities to nonhuman entities. She describes how Death "kindly stopped for me" and "knew no haste." She also uses human pronouns, such as "He" and "We," and human actions, such as "drove," "knew," and "paused." The poem's speaker even sets aside their "labor and [their] leisure too" to be polite to death. Analogy (A) is a comparison of different things that have some common attribute, like saying that the human heart is like a pump. The poem does analogize (for example, by describing a house that is really a grave), but the poem as a whole describes death using personification. Hyperbole (B) is extreme exaggeration, which there is no use of here. Alliteration (C) is repetition of sounds in adjacent or close words. Although the poem contains some uses of alliteration, such as "Gazing Grain" and "Setting Sun," the overall description of death uses personification.

118. C: While the topic of this poem is death, the tone is lighthearted, and the poem finds humor in death with a gentle kind of irony, so choice C is correct. The diction, word choice, rhythms, and conclusion do not convey gravity or darkness (A). The descriptive details of the journey to eternity, slow yet seemingly over within a day in retrospect, do not convey detachment, alienation, or numbness (B). Rather, the persona in the poem seems to go on a pleasant journey with death and quietly observes Death's "kindly" character and "Civility"—examples of the gentle irony that the poet uses here. The deliberate, placid narrative has no frantic, agitated, frenzied, or fearful (D) qualities.

119. B: The fifth stanza, about "a House that seemed/A Swelling of the Ground," is an oblique description of a grave. Its cornice is "in the Ground" and the roof is "scarcely visible," indicating that this "House" is underground. This is not a literal description of a home (A) or a church (C). A school (D) with children at recess is described as one of the aspects of life they pass in their journey, in the third stanza. The fifth stanza's description of a grave is in keeping with the whole poem's light, gentle, indirect, and accepting treatment of death.

120. B: Students must be able to distinguish between printed words and the spaces between them to identify the first and last letters of each word, as spaces are the boundaries between words. It is not true that all normally developing students can tell words from spaces: those not exposed to or familiar with print media may need to be taught this distinction. Although left-to-right directionality is more of a problem for ELL students whose L1s have different writing or printing directions (e.g., some Asian languages are written vertically, some can be written vertically or horizontally, and some Semitic languages like Hebrew and Arabic are written right-to-left), again, children unfamiliar with print or writing may also not know writing, print, or book directionality either. Identifying basic punctuation is important to reading comprehension as it affects meaning. For example, consider "Let's eat, Grandma" vs. "Let's eat Grandma"—one comma differentiates an invitation to dinner from a cannibalistic proposal.

121. A: Literal language, which says just what it means, is analogous to denotation, which is the literal meaning of a word (or its dictionary definition). Figurative language, which adds meaning beyond the literal meaning, is analogous to connotation, which involves ideas associated with a word beyond its literal definition. Choice B is incorrect because some types of informational text, such as advertisements, have a purpose that is well-served by figurative language. Choice C is incorrect because there is no requirement to use figurative language in informational text. Choice D is incorrect because informational text can use figurative language and connotations, just as narrative writing does.

122. A: Text coding and monitoring uses eight codes for students to annotate informational text they read. Four of those codes are included in these choices. Choice A is correct because the "??" code means "I am really confused about this part." The other choices refer to valid codes that have other meanings. The "?" code (B) means "I have a question about this part." The "L" code (C) means "I learned something new from this part." And the "RR" code (D) means "I need to reread this part."

123. A: Choice A is correct because a writer must use the body of the essay to argue for the thesis. This argument is the main content of the essay, and it can be seen as the only reason for writing a whole essay rather than just a thesis statement. Choice B is incorrect because clarifying the meanings of unfamiliar words should be done in the body of the essay, but it should not be the primary focus of the body. Choice C is incorrect because this purpose should be achieved in the conclusion of the essay. Choice D is incorrect because a writer's aim when writing an essay should not be to use specific facts to make generalizations.

124. D: *Although Ted had an impressive education* is a dependent or subordinate clause, introduced by the subordinating conjunction *although* and modifying the independent clause *he had little work experience*. The second dependent clause is the relative clause *which presented a challenge during his job search*, introduced by the relative pronoun *which* and modifying *he had little work experience*. Thus, there are two dependent clauses and one independent clause, so Choice D is correct.

125. A: The haiku, originating in Japanese poetry and since adopted in English-language poetry, is a short poem of only three lines, often with 17 syllables, with the first and third lines having five syllables and the second line having seven syllables. (In Japanese there are many other rules, which become complicated in comparison to the English version.) Because this syllable pattern is a defining characteristic of English-language haiku, choice A is correct. Haiku are typically unrhymed, so they do not have a rhyme scheme (B). Similarly, they do not employ any regular meter (C). Because haiku are typically 17 syllables or fewer, they do not involve long narratives (D).

126. C: It is most appropriate for students to write using more casual language on their own age level when writing for classmates. This applies whether they are writing narrative, argumentation, exposition, or speculation. When students want to share a particular experience with their readers (A), they should write using descriptive form, rather than persuasive or explanatory form, for example. Age/reading level will be determined by the audience. When students want permission for a desired activity (B), they should write using persuasive form, with mature, serious diction and more sophisticated vocabulary to appeal to parents. To write a story that younger children can read (D), they should write in narrative form, using simpler vocabulary and sentence structure; shorter sentences; more vivid, entertaining word choices; a lighter tone; and humor when appropriate.

127. C: Focusing each paragraph on one main idea (A) contributes to writing good paragraphs. The writer may state this idea overtly in a topic sentence, or simply imply a more obvious main topic that readers can infer. Giving specific details to develop that main idea (B) is also a practice that results in better paragraphs. However, it is not true that the more details, the better (C): excessive details will destroy the paragraph's focus and confuse readers. Another practice for developing good paragraphs is using specific structural patterns (D), e.g., comparison–contrast, division and classification, analogy, cause-and-effect, definition, description, narration, process, or example and illustration.

128. D: It is impossible to include every text desired into the language curriculum—there are simply too many good books, stories, poems, speeches, and media available. Teachers must first think about what skills their students need to acquire, as well as what skills they have already mastered. In designing activities for class, a good teacher will start first with the purpose for instruction. For example, purposes of reading can include: reading for information, reading for enjoyment, understanding a message, identifying main or supporting ideas, or developing an appreciation for artistic expression/perception. Once the purpose or intended learning outcome has been identified, the teacher will have a much better idea of which texts, strategies, and activities will support that purpose.

129. D: Relating stories of fictional characters is not a typical purpose of journal writing, so choice D is correct. Although a narrative may be written in the form of journal entries that are imagined to be written by a character in the narrative, such writing is still narrative writing, and not genuine journaling. The other choices each refer to a common purpose of journal writing. Each of these three options are generally introspective subjects someone might write about so they can remember it in more detail later or keep track of how far they have come.

130. B: Typical speech is roughly 125 words per minute, while typical thinking is estimated at roughly 500 words per minute. This natural disparity does not make listening less effective than reading. While the slower rate of speech and the faster rate of thought does allow students' minds to wander, teachers can have students make use of this time by instructing them to summarize mentally the speech they hear as an active listening technique. This enables students to process, consider, and manipulate heard information and make richer, more creative decisions about it. Listening and learning share the common characteristics of being both social and reciprocal.